JACK DAVIS was born in Perth in 1917 and brought up at Yarloop and the Moore River native settlements. He first began to learn the language and culture of his people, the Nyoongarah of South-West of Western Australia, while living on the Brookton Aboriginal Reserve. He later worked as a stockman in the North-West which brought him into contact with tribal society.

He became an activist on behalf of his people and from 1967–71 was director of the Aboriginal Centre in Perth. In 1971 he became the first chairman of the Aboriginal Trust in West Australia and from 1972–77 was managing editor of the Aboriginal Publications Foundation. He was a member of the Institute of Aboriginal Studies in Canberra and established a course for Aboriginal writers at Murdoch University. He was also a member of the Aboriginal Arts Board of the Australia Council.

His first full-length play, *Kullark*, a documentary on the history of Aboriginals in West Australia, was first presented in 1979. It was followed by *The Dreamers* (1983), which toured Australia under the auspices of the Australian Elizabethan Theatre Trust. Following the success of this tour, the Trust commissioned *No Sugar* for the 1985 Festival of Perth and *Honey Spot*, a children's play, for the 1985 Come Out Festival in Adelaide. In 1986 *No Sugar* was remounted by the Trust for a season at the World Theatre Festival in Vancouver.

For services to his people Jack Davis received the British Empire Medal in 1977; in 1985 he became a member of the Order of Australia, received the Sydney Myer Performing Arts Award, an Hon. D.Litt from Murdoch University and was elected Citizen of the Year in West Australia. In 1986 *No Sugar* was co-winner of the Australian Writers Guild award for the best stage play of the year.

Jack Davis died in March 2000.

Morton Hansen as Sam in the Western Australian Theatre Company production, Vancouver and Melbourne 1986. Photo by Tony McDonough.

No Sugar

Jack Davis

CURRENCY PRESS, SYDNEY

CURRENCY PLAYS
First published in 1986 by
Currency Press Pty Ltd
PO Box 2287
Strawberry Hills NSW 2012
www.currency.com.au
enquiries@currency.com.au

Reprinted 1988, 1990, 1991, 1993, 1994, 1995, 1996, 1998, 1999, 2000, 2002 (twice), 2003, 2004, 2006, 2007, 2009, 2010, 2012, 2013, 2014 (twice), 2015, 2016, 2019, 2020, 2021

NATIONAL LIBRARY OF AUSTRALIA CIP DATA
Davis, Jack, 1917–2000
    No Sugar
    Bibliography
    ISBN 9780868191461
    1. Aborigines, Australian—Drama. 1.Title
    (Series: Currency Plays).
    A822.3

Cover: Dorothy Collard as Gran in the Australian Elizabethan Theatre Trust production. Photo by Tony McDonough
Typeset by Emily Ralph for Currency Press.
Printed by CanPrint Communications.

Publication of this title was assisted by the Commonwealth Government through the Australia Council, its arts funding and advisory body.

Contents

Director Andrew Ross addressing the audience at the Maltings, Perth. Photo by Tony McDonough.

Foreword

The unique collaboration and friendship between Jack Davis and Andrew Ross dates back to 1979 when Andrew directed Jack's first play, *Kuflask*, which toured extensively in Western Australia for the Perth Playhouse Company. By 1982 the Swan River Stage Company had been formed and Jack Davis's second play *The Dreamers* was seen at that year's Festival of Perth.

The production was such an important step in the history of Aboriginal drama that the Australian Elizabethan Theatre Trust toured the Playhouse Company's re-production for seventeen weeks around Australia. For many of the cast of ten it was the first time out of their home State, but they adapted to venues as different as the Sydney Opera House and the historic Theatre Royal in Hobart.

It was important that more Australians, and indeed the world, had an opportunity to learn about Aboriginality through the words of this amazing storyteller; so in 1984 the AETT commissioned two more plays with the support of the Department of Aboriginal Affairs and the Literature Board of the Australia Council. The result was *Honey Spot*, a play for children that deals with the issues of race relations and the conservation of our environment; and *No Sugar*. *No Sugar* tells the story of a family's fight for survival during the Depression years and was staged in a semi-promenade setting in which the audience followed the players on their journey through the action of the play.

The first season of *No Sugar*, directed by Andrew Ross and presented as the inaugural production of the newly-formed Western Australian Theatre Company in association with the Trust, was an exciting success at the 1985 Festival of Perth. The production was seen by the producer of the World Theatre Festival and this resulted in an invitation to represent Australia at Vancouver's Expo '86. Performing alongside the Beijing People's Art Theatre from China and the Kirov Ballet from the USSR, *No Sugar* proved a sell-out success and received a standing ovation from its audience. After a further season as guests of the National Arts Centre in Ottawa the Company returned to Melbourne to promenade with an equally responsive audience around the grand old Fitzroy Town Hall.

Wendy Blacklock
Director, Australian Content Department
Australian Elizabethan Theatre Trust, Sydney

Jack Davis as Billy and Richard Walley as Bluey relive the Oombulgarri massacre in the W.A. Theatre Company production. Photo by Tony McDonough.

Left: from the original production, Jedda Cole as Mary with John Pell as Joe; and Ernie Dingo as Billy. Photos by David Cruse. Above: Dorothy Collard as Gran. Photo by Tony McDonough.

No Sugar was first performed by the Playhouse Company in association with the Australian Elizabethan Theatre Trust at the Maltings, North Perth, for the Festival of Perth on 18 February 1985 with the following cast:

JIMMY	Jim Holland
GRAN	Dorothy Collard
MILLY	Lynette Narkle
SAM	Morton Hansen
JOE	John Pell
CISSIE	Lynley Narkle
DAVID	Kelton Pell
FRANK BROWN	Shane McNamara
SERGEANT CARROL	Bill McCluskey
CONSTABLE KERR	Shane McNamara
JUSTICE OF PEACE	Dibbs Mather
MR A.O. NEVILLE	Dibbs Mather
MISS DUNN	Annie O'Shannessey
MR N.S. NEAL	Bill McCluskey
MATRON NEAL	Sally Sander
TOPSY	Charmaine Cole
TURVY	Brooke Michael
SISTER EILEEN	Annie O'Shannessy
MARY	Jedda Cole
BILLY	Ernie Dingo
BLUEY	Richard Walley
PETER	Colin Kickett
DANCER	Colin Kickett
MUSICIAN	Richard Walley

Directed by Andrew Ross
Designed by Steve Nolan
Choreography and music by Richard Walley

The play was then revised and remounted for participation in the Expo '86 World Theatre Festival in Vancouver. This version was first performed on 15 May 1986 at the West End Community Centre, Vancouver, with the following cast:

JIMMY	Ernie Dingo
GRAN	Dorothy Mallard
MILLY	Lynette Narkle
SAM	Morton Hansen
JOE	John Pell
CISSIE	Lynley Narkle
DAVID	Kelton Pell
FRANK BROWN	Shane McNamara
SERGEANT CARROL	Ben Gabriel
CONSTABLE KERR	Shane McNamara
JUSTICE OF THE PEACE	James Beattie
MR A.O. NEVILLE	James Beattie
MISS DUNN	Annie O'Shannessy
MR N.S. NEAL	Ben Gabriel
MATRON NEAL	Doreen Warburton
TOPSY	Charmaine Cole
SISTER EILEEN	Annie O'Shannessy
MARY	Jedda Cole
BILLY	Jack Davis
BLUEY	Richard Walley

Directed by Andrew Ross
Designed by Steve Nolan
Choreography and music by Richard Walley

CHARACTERS

JIMMY MUNDAY

GRAN MUNDAY, Jimmy's mother

MILLY MILLIMURRA, Jimmy's sister

SAM MILLIMURRA, Milly's husband

JOE MILLIMURRA, their eldest son

CASSIE MILLIMURRA, their daughter

DAVID MILLIMURRA, their younger son

FRANK BROWN, an unemployed father

SERGEANT CARROL, sergeant of police at Northam

CONSTABLE KERR, of the Northam Police

JUSTICE OF THE PEACE, a Northam cocky father

AUBER OCTAVIUS NEVILLE, Chief Protector of Aboriginies

MISS DUNN, his secretary

MR N.S. NEAL, Superintendent of the Moore River Settlement

MATRON NEAL, (*Koodjie*) his wife, matron in charge of the
    Settlement hospital

TOPSY, a Settlement girl, assisting matron

SISTER EILEEN, a missionary

MARY DARGURRU, a young girl from the Kimberly region

BILLY KIMBERLY, a black tracker

BLUEY, a black tracker

SETTING

The play is designed for a dispersed setting on an open stage. On one side is the Avon Valley town of Northam, including the Police Station with two cells, a main street and the Government Well Aboriginal Reserve. Also on this side should be the office, in Murray Street, Perth, of the Chief Protector of Aborigines, with an entrance front and rear for whites and blacks respectively. The scene on the other side is the Moore River Native Settlement, near Mogumber in the Victoria Plains district. The areas include the Superintendent's office, the Millimurra tent and camp at Long Pool, a clearing in the pine plantation and a dais and flagpole. Other parts of the stage serve as an area by the railway line at Moolumbeenee and a meeting room of the Western Australian Historical Society.

ACT ONE, NORTHAM

SCENE ONE

Government Well Aboriginal Reserve, Northam, morning, 1929. SAM
MILLIMURRA *prepares mugs of tea, lacing them generously with sugar.
He passes one to* JOE *who is absorbed in the special centenary edition
of the Western Mail.* GRAN *and* MILLY *sort clothes for washing.* DAVID
and CISSIE *play cricket with a home-made bat and ball.* JIMMY *sharpens
an axe, bush fashion.*

DAVID: Bowl overarm!

CISSIE: I can't.

DAVID: Well, try.

> *She does, clumsily.* JOE *bashes the paper into shape and reads
> aloud falteringly. His father,* SAM, *listens with great interest.*

JOE: 'The— blood— was stirred as if by a trumpet… by the historical…

> CISSIE *bowls again.* DAVID *bashes the ball out of sight.*

DAVID: *Woolah!* Don Bradman.

> DAVID *and* CISSIE *scamper after the ball.*

JOE:… Headed by a tableau…

MILLY: David, where you goin'? Gimme that shirt, it's filthy.

> DAVID *removes it and inspects it but continues after the ball. He
> and* CISSIE *exit.*

JOE:… Commemorating the pioneers whose lives…

GRAN: [*to* JIMMY] James, you put that bucket a' water on?

JIMMY: Yeah, Mum, boilin' and waitin' for you by now.

JOE:… Were a steadfast performance of duty in the face of difficulty
and danger. With them was a reminder of the dangers they faced, in
the shape of three lorries… carrying Aborigines.

> *They all stop what they are doing and listen.*

Aborigines, incong… incongruously…

SAM: Come on.

JOE: All right! '… Dancing… to a brass band.'

SAM *laughs.*

SAM: *Koorawoorung*! Nyoongahs corroboreein' to a *wetjala*'s brass band!

JIMMY: Ah! That beats everythin': stupid bloody blackfellas.

GRAN: Ay! You… *dawarra* you *mirri* up and get them clothes down the soak, go on!

JIMMY *gets up, but can't resist the final word.*

JIMMY: You fellas, you know why them *wetjalas* marchin' down the street, eh? I'll tell youse why. 'Cause them bastards took our country and them blackfellas dancin' for 'em. Bastards!

He nicks his finger with the axe and watches the blood drip to the ground. GRAN *gives him a piece of cloth for it.*

MILLY: Don't worry, if you woulda been there you woulda been right with 'em.

JIMMY: No bloody fear I wouldn't have.

He drives the axe savagely into a log.

GRAN: Eh! Now you take them clothes down the soak, you 'ear me?

JIMMY *reluctantly obeys,* DAVID *and* CISSIE *return with the bat but no ball.* DAVID *wears his shirt inside out.*

DAVID: You're the fielder; you're supposed to chase it.

CISSIE: Well, you shouldn't hit it so hard.

DAVID: Yeah, well it's lost now.

MILLY: Come on, you two, get to school.

Reaching into a pocket.

Here's twopence, you can buy an apple each for lunch.

She gives it to them.

DAVID: Aw, can't I have enough for a pie?

MILLY: It's all the money I got.

CISSIE: Aw mum, Old Tony the ding always sells us little shrivelled ones and them *wetjala* kids big fat ones.

JOE: Here's thrippence each.

JOE *flips them sixpence.*

DAVID: Aw, thanks, Brudge.

MILLY: Where's that shirt?

DAVID: [*tapping his chest*] 'Ere.

MILLY: Take it off.

DAVID: But it's clean on this side.

MILLY: Come 'ere.

> *She tugs it off him and swaps it for a clean one.*

And you go straight down the soak after school. [*To* SAM *and* JOE] And you fellas, we got no meat for dinner or supper; you'll have to go out and get a couple of rabbits.

> GRAN *and* MILLY *exit.* JOE *continues to read to himself.*

SAM: Ba, ba, what else?

JOE: 'The pag... page... page – ant pre – sented a picture of Western Australia's pre-sent condition of hopeful optimum – optimistic prosperity, and gave some idea of what men mean when they talk about the soul of the nation.'

SAM: Sounds like bullshit to me. Come on, let's get these rabbits.

> JOE *springs to his feet and walks off. Dogs bark.*

Bring Ruffy and Moonie; don't bring Spring, he's too slow.

> JOE *returns with a dowak. He picks up the camp oven.*

JOE: *Allewah wilbra, gnuny barminy barkiny.*

> *He mimes throwing the doak at a rabbit and runs off after his father.*

SCENE TWO

A street in Northam, day. FRANK BROWN *rolls a cigarette from stoopers.* SERGEANT CARROL *enters from the police station and approaches him.*

SERGEANT: Hey, just a moment you!

FRANK: Yes?

SERGEANT: How long you been in Northam?

FRANK: About a fortnight.

SERGEANT: Where are you camped?

FRANK: Down near the saleyards.

SERGEANT: By yourself?

FRANK: No, there's about ten other blokes.

SERGEANT: White blokes?

FRANK: What?

SERGEANT: Not abos or half-castes?

FRANK: No, why?

SERGEANT: Your name Francis Brown?

FRANK: Yes.

SERGEANT: You've been seen hangin' about with natives.

FRANK: It's not against the law.

SERGEANT: No, Mr Brown, it's not, but it is an offence to supply liquor to an Aboriginal native under the Aboriginal Act.

FRANK: Thanks for the information.

SERGEANT: Oh I've got plenty of information, mate. Last Friday, James Munday, a native, took a bundle of fox scalps to the Shire Office and collected a bounty of three pounds.

FRANK: Very interesting. And?

SERGEANT: And, on Friday night he was apprehended drunk in Bernard Park after you were seen purchasing two bottles of port wine in the Shamrock Hotel.

FRANK: I'm a wine connoissuer.

SERGEANT: [*intimately*] Listen, mate, don't try being smart. This time I sent Munday back to his camp with a warning; next time I'll nail him and the bloke that buys wine for him. The last bloke I nabbed for supplying is doing three months hard labour in Fremantle.

FRANK: Thanks for the tip.

SERGEANT: Why don't you think about movin' on?

FRANK: Where to? I been on the road already for six months. Kondinin, Merredin, Kalgoorlie: no work. Headed up the Murchison, Mullewa, Northampton: nothing. I got a wife and two kids staying with her parents in Leederville. I can't even raise a train fare to Perth to go and see them.

> The SERGEANT *takes out a packet of cigarettes and gives a couple to* FRANK.

SERGEANT: Look, mate, I understand; I hear it every day a' the week, but I got a job to do, so don't forget what I said.

FRANK: Thanks.

SERGEANT: Natives best left to keep to themselves.

FRANK: I was only tryin' to do—

SERGEANT: [*interrupting*] You might think your doin' 'em a good turn, but you're not. Take it from me, I been dealin' with 'em for years. I got nothin' against 'em, but I know exactly what they're like.

FRANK *carefully puts the cigarettes away as the* SERGEANT *enters the police station.* MISS DUNN *enters an office with a sign displayed, reading 'Government of Western Australia, Fisheries, Forestry, Wildlife and Aborigines'. There are two desks, each with a telephone. She goes immediately to one, takes a note from her handbag and dials.* FRANK *exits. The* SERGEANT *settles behind his desk and busies himself.*

MISS DUNN: [*into the receiver*] Hell... Hello, good morning. Is that the West? Yes, thankyou... I'd like to place an advertisement, 'Wanted to Sell'.

NEVILLE *enters. He takes some files from his briefcase and settles down at his desk with the West Australian.*

NEVILLE: Good Morning, Miss Dunn.

MISS DUNN: [*into the receiver*] A motorcycle. [*To* NEVILLE] Good morning, Mr Neville. I'm sorry, it's a personal... [*into the receiver*] sorry. Twelve pounds, in, Douglas, 1923 Model, one forty-eight Stirling Street, Highgate... Please. [*To* NEVILLE] Sorry, Mr Neville, it's a personal call... [*Into the receiver*] Thankyou... Dunn... Miss E.

NEVILLE: I didn't know you were a motorcyclist.

MISS DUNN: No, it's my brother's. He's down the South West, looking for work, and his wife and children are with me.

NEVILLE: Couldn't find anything in Perth.

MISS DUNN: No, and not for want of trying. He eventually got work selling wirelesses. Door to door.

NEVILLE: Doesn't sound very suitable.

MISS DUNN: He only sold one in three weeks, didn't even cover the cost of the petrol.

NEVILLE: Well, he's certainly not on his own. Unemployment's hit thirty per cent according to the *West.*

MISS DUNN: There's some mail for you, and an urgent internal one from the Minister's Office and one from the Northam Town Clerk.

NEVILLE: Goodness me, the *West*'s scraping the barrel for a bit of good news. Results of the 'Most Economical Housewife Contest'... What next?... I'm afraid you're not the lucky winner, Miss Dunn.

He shows her the paper.

MISS DUNN: 'Mrs Hill of Greenmount on two pounds five shillings a week... ' Rent, seven shillings; light, one and threepence.

MISS DUNN reads to herself.

NEVILLE: She's ingenious, alright: makes tap washers out of old car tyres.

MISS DUNN: Yes, and slippers from her husband's old felt hats.

NEVILLE picks up the mail and starts to read it.

NEVILLE: Perhaps the West could run a contest for the most frugal civil servant... Could you get me Sergeant Carrol in Northam on the line, please?

He gets out files and makes notes while MISS DUNN dials the exchange.

MISS DUNN: Trunks please... Hello... Northam nine please... Yes, BM nine-seven-oh-seven... Thankyou operator.

She hangs up.

NEVILLE: Can you take down a note for the Minister, please?

He shuffles through the files and documents.

My dear Minister, herewith the information requested. I know I don't need to remind your good self of the extreme budgetry constraints under which this Department operates. Item one: the native weekly ration currently costs this Department two shillings and fourpence per week. Perhaps this bears comparison with the sustenance paid to white unemployed which I believe is seven shillings per week.

The phone rings in the Northam Police Station. SERGEANT CARROL answers it.

SERGEANT: Hello, Northam Police Station. Thanks, Sybil.

NEVILLE: Item two: off the cuff, the proposed budget cut of three thousand one hundred and thirty-four pounds could be met by discontinuing the supply of meat in native rations. Soap was discontinued this financial year. Item Three: of eighty girls from the Moore River Native Settlement who went out into domestic service last year, thirty returned—

The phone rings in NEVILLE*'s office.* MISS DUNN *picks up the receiver.*

MISS DUNN: Excuse me, Mr Neville… [*Into the receiver*] Hello, Chief Protector of Aborigines Office… Thankyou, operator. [*To* NEVILLE] Northam.

NEVILLE *takes the call and* MISS DUNN *hangs up.*

NEVILLE: Sergeant Carrol. Neville, Aborigines.

SERGEANT: Hello, Northam Police… Hello.

NEVILLE: It's an awful line, Sergeant. Are you on the line?

SERGEANT: Yes, I can hear you.

NEVILLE: Good. We seem to have encountered a few obstacles with the new reserve. The Guilford Road site isn't acceptable to the Council. Apparently the adjoining landholders have lodged objections.

SERGEANT: I thought they might. What grounds? Did they say?

NEVILLE: [*looking at his letter*] A Mr Smith…

NEVILLE: Oh, yeah.

NEVILLE:… Claims he wouldn't be able to go out and leave his wife home alone at night.

SERGEANT: And he's generally down the Shamrock Hotel till stumps.

GRAN *and* MILLY *approach the Police Station.*

NEVILLE: Well, the upshot of it is that the Lands Department won't be able to gazette it, so you as the local Protector of Aborigines will have to recommend an alternative site… The Council's concerned that it's well away from any residences.

GRAN: Chergeant!… Chergeant!

NEVILLE: What's that terrible racket?

GRAN: Chergeant!

SERGEANT: [*to* NEVILLE] Ration day.

GRAN: Chergeant.

NEVILLE: All right, letter to follow, I'll leave you to it.

SERGEANT: Thanks, Mr Neville.

NEVILLE: Cheerio.

The SERGEANT *and* NEVILLE *hang up.*

SERGEANT: Alright Gran, come in.

NEVILLE: Where was I?

MISS DUNN: Of eighty who went out in the domestic service last year...

NEVILLE: Thirty returned to the settlement in pregnant condition, yours etcetera... If you could type that straight away I'll run it up to the Office myself.

The SERGEANT *places flour, sugar and two small packages on the bench and marks them off in his ration book.*

SERGEANT: Flour, sugar, tea... And how you been keepin', Granny?

GRAN: I'm awright.

SERGEANT: Been behavin' yourself?

GRAN: Have you?

SERGEANT: There's your butcher's order, meat and dripping.

MILLY: [*inspecting the small packages*] You got two cream a tartar 'ere.

SERGEANT: Right, let's change 'em.

GRAN: Damper won't rise without no bicarbonate.

SERGEANT: That shouldn't worry you, Granny, you should remember when you used to grind up jam and wattle seeds.

GRAN: More better than white man's flour, no weevils in jam and wattle seeds.

SERGEANT: Good tucker, eh?

GRAN: When I was that high we go and get 'em and smash 'em up and get a bag full, that much!

SERGEANT: You can still collect 'em, nothin' stoppin' you.

GRAN: Where? *Wetjala* cut all the trees down.

MILLY: Haven't got any soap yet.

SERGEANT: I'm afraid that soap is no longer included as a ration item.

MILLY: What do you mean, we got no more soap?

SERGEANT: That's right.

MILLY: But why? What am I gonna wash with? How can I keep my kids clean and sen 'em to school?

SERGEANT: You could buy some.

MILLY: What with?

GRAN: What about *gnummarri*? You stop that too?

SERGEANT: No, Granny, you still get your stick of nigger twist.

He gives it to her.

MILLY: Whose idea was it to stop the soap?

SERGEANT: The idea, as you call it, came from the Aboriginal Department in Perth.

GRAN: Mister Neville?

MILLY: I just can't believe it: no soap!

SERGEANT: Your trouble, Milly, is you got three healthy men bludging off you, too lazy to work.

MILLY: Where they gonna get work?

SERGEANT: They're afraid to look for it in case they find it.

MILLY: Cockies want 'em to work for nothin'.

GRAN: They not slaves, Chergeant!

SERGEANT: Well, they'll have to work if you want luxury items like soap.

MILLY: Look, last week my Joe cut a hundred posts for old Skinny Martin and you know what he got? A pair of second-hand boots and a piece of stag ram so tough even the dawgs couldn't eat it; skinnier than old Martin 'imself.

GRAN: And we couldn't eat the boots.

MILLY: You wait till brother Jimmy hears about this no soap business. He'll make you fellas jump.

SERGEANT: Yeah, and you tell that bush lawyer brother of yours, if he comes here arguing I'll make him jump: straight inside.

They turn to go. As they leave he raises his voice after them.

You hear me?

MILLY: [*calling*] Yeah, I hear you. Can't help hearin' you.

They walk down the street.

GRAN: [*calling*] You don't want to shout like that, Chergeant. You'll 'ave a fit, just like a dingo when he gets bait.

MILLY: [*calling*] Seein' you're drinkin down the Federal every night, Sergeant, you can tell old Skinny Martin to stick his stag ram right up his skinny *kwon*!

GRAN: [*calling*] Yeah, an' the boots too.

They exit, laughing and hooting Nyoongah fashion. The SERGEANT *returns to the police station, puts the ration book away and settles down to reading the newspaper.* MISS DUNN *finishes typing the letter. She hands it to* NEVILLE, *who reads it quickly.*

NEVILLE: [*signing it*] Thankyou, Miss Dunn. We'd better get a thankyou note off to Mr Neal.

MISS DUNN: I can do it straight away for you.

NEVILLE: All right; Mr N.S. Neal, Superintendent, Moore River Native Settlement, etcetera.

Dear Mr Neal, just a short note to thank you for your... thank you and Matron for your hospitality on our recent visit to the Settlement. The Settlement is looking splendid, considering, obviously a credit to you both. The conduct of the ceremony was a tribute to your military precision, and the afternoon tea, especially Matron's home-made lemonade, was splendid on such a hot day. As I mentioned, I was a little concerned to see so many dirty little noses amongst the children. I'm a great believer that if you provide the native the basic accoutrements of civilisation you're half way to civilising him. I'd like to see each child issued with a handkerchief and instructed on its use. Funds as always are short so I've taken the liberty of ordering several bolts of cloth from Government stores. I'm sure the girls in the sewing room could run up the handkerchiefs. I take your point about losing them and suggest attaching them to their sleeves by way of a tape. Likewise, as discussed, the stores branch will henceforth be supplying limited supplies of toilet paper for use in the dormitory lavatories. I think some practical training from yourself and Matron in its correct usage would be appropriate. If you can successfully inculcate such basic but essential details of civilised living you will have helped them along the road to taking their place in Australian society. Again, many thanks to Matron and yourself. Australia Day at the settlement is something I'll always look forward to.

Yours, etcetera.

I'd better get this off to the Minister. I'll be back after lunch.

SCENE THREE

Government Well, dusk. Magpies are carolling. CISSIE *is preparing a damper.* JOE *and* DAVID *play two-up with bottle tops.* DAVID *has the headers.*

DAVID: Come on, set me up. Not beer tops, wine tops.

CISSIE: [*calling*] Joe! Make a place for the damper for me.

JOE: [*laughing, to* DAVID] Don't make no difference.

DAVID: It does.

JOE: Why?

DAVID: Wine cost more than beer.

CISSIE: Joe! Joe, come on.

JOE: Okay. Okay.

> CISSIE *calls impatiently. The dough is beginning to fall apart.*

CISSIE: Joe, hurry up!

JOE: Awright.

CISSIE: Joe, come on!

> CISSIE *stands by the fire holding the dough.* JOE *uses his doak to make an impression in the ashes.* CISSIE *puts the damper in and covers it with ashes.*

DAVID: [*spinning*] *Woolah!* Heads!

JOE: Let's have a look.

DAVID: *Moorditj, unna?*

> *The dogs bark.*

CISSIE: David, git me some more wood. [DAVID *spins.*] David!

DAVID: Wait till I've finished spinnin'.

CISSIE: *Shoo-i*, tail them.

> DAVID *spins them high.*

DAVID: Have a look at them, Ciss.

> *He looks. They're tails.*

See what you made me do.

> *He goes for the wood.*

CISSIE: Joe, better chop some more wood up.

JOE: Yeah, okay.

> *He spins.*

Bastard.

> *He picks up the axe and goes to the woodpile.* DAVID *returns with a load of wood. He puts it down and begins to count his bottle tops.*

DAVID: Boy, look at my *boondah.*

> JIMMY *enters.*

JIMMY: Wait till I see him tomorrow. I'll give him no soap.

SAM *and* FRANK *follows* JIMMY. *The men are slightly drunk.*
Finally, GRAN *and* MILLY *enter.*

CISSIE: About time.

DAVID: Took youse long enough, got any boiled lollies?

GRAN: No. No lollies.

MILLY: Ain't even got no soap.

JOE: [*indicating* FRANK] *Gneean baal?*

JIMMY: He's our friend.

SAM: Ay! Mate! That's me eldest boy Joe, and that's Cissie and that's the youngest, David.

FRANK: Hello.

The children don't reply.

CISSIE: Ay, Mum? Why isn't there any soap? I wanna wash my hair tomorrow.

GRAN: What you got in the camp oven?

She looks.

MILLY: Don't git soap in the rations no more.

GRAN: [*Peering into the camp oven*] No onions or taters.

CISSIE: Why? What for?

She feels her hair.

MILLY: Just what I said, darlin', Sergeant ain't giving no soap any more.

GRAN: Don't worry, we can use *tjeerung* bush. I know where some growin'.

JIMMY: Don't worry about Sergeant, I'll give him a piece of my mind.

GRAN: You know what he'll give you? Six months.

JIMMY *takes a drink.*

JIMMY: Six months.

He laughs.

Mother, I can do that standing on my head.

He passes the bottle to FRANK.

Here, mate.

DAVID: Ay, Dad, fixed my bike today. Wanna see it?

SAM: Yeah.

DAVID *runs off, followed by* CISSIE.

DAVID: It's goin' real good.

GRAN *puts onions and potatoes in the camp oven.* JIMMY
produces turnips from his pocket.

JIMMY: Here, Mum, chuck them in.

MILLY: Ay! Where d'you git them from?

JOE: He never growed 'em and I bet he never bought 'em.

MILLY *takes them, prepares them and adds them to the rabbit
stew.* JIMMY *produces a mouth organ.*

MILLY: You lookin' for gaol awright!

JIMMY: [*to* FRANK] You been inside?

FRANK: Inside? Inside where?

JIMMY: Gaol. You been in Freeo?

FRANK: No.

GRAN: You'll be in gaol if Chergeant catch you here.

SAM: Ne'mine 'bout Sergeant, Mother-In-Law; give him a feed.

MILLY: Won't be long; stew ain't proper cooked yet.

JIMMY *takes a drink.*

JIMMY: Ay *wetjala.* You know how many time I been in gaol? [*Holding
up four fingers*] That many times.

FRANK: [*shyly*] What for?

JIMMY: Aw, drinkin', fightin' and snowdroppin'.

SAM: You know what snowdroppin' is?

MILLY: Pinchin' things off other people's clothes lines.

JIMMY: Hey, *wetjala*, mate, you know when I was a little fella, 'bout
twelve, thirteen years old...

JOE: Aw, here we go...

JIMMY Shut up, you. [*To* FRANK] You know what I was?

FRANK: Ah, no.

JIMMY: Choir boy. I tell you I was the leadin' choir boy at New Norcia
Mission; wasn't I, Mother?

SAM: Didn't do you much good.

MILLY: He used to sing 'Ave Maria' solo, real good.

JIMMY: Yeah! [*To* SAM] 'Ow do you know? You wasn't even there.

SAM: 'Course I was there. [*To* FRANK] That's where I met her, *unna* Mill?

FRANK: Did you get married at New Norcia?

SAM: Too right.

GRAN: In the church too.

JIMMY: An' engaged under a Government blanket.

MILLY: Shut up! *Dawarra, nitja wetjala.*

GRAN: [*clicking her tongue*] *Choo, kienya.*

JIMMY: I'm only jokin'. Anyways, who wants to 'ear a song?

> JIMMY *produces a mouth organ and plays 'Springtime in the Rockies'.* MILLY *begins to remove the damper from the ashes and dust it off.*

MILLY: Cissie! David! Mum, see if the stew's cooked... Cissie! David!

> GRAN *checks the stew.*

GRAN: Yeah, it's cooked.

> CISSIE *and* DAVID *return with the bike.* JOE *spreads a wogga on the ground.*

Cissie, plates, plates. David, put the billy on.

DAVID: Me bike's *moorditj*; we went right down the rubbish dump.

CISSIE: Yeah, an' I had to push you back through the sand.

> DAVID *lays the bike on its side and they sit and serve the food.* SAM *breaks up the damper.*

SAM: [*to* FRANK] You eat this before?

FRANK: Damper? Plenty a' times.

SAM: Cooked in the ashes?

FRANK: No.

JOE: You eat underground mutton before?

> MILLY *gives him a plate of stew.*

FRANK: What? Oh, thanks, missus.

JIMMY: Underground mutton!

JOE: Rabbit.

JIMMY: You try that, dip the damper, *moorditj*!

FRANK: Yeah, we used to live on 'em when we was on the farm.

GRAN: James, you come an' get your supper.

JIMMY: No, leave it, I'll get it dreckly.

He takes a long drink of wine as the others eat.

[*To* GRAN *and* MILLY*, indicating* FRANK] You see that fella there, Mum, Mill? He had his own farm once. You wouldn't believe it, eh?

JOE: [*to* FRANK] Yeah? Where?

FRANK: Out Lake Yealering.

JOE: What happened?

FRANK: Aw, between the rabbits and a couple of bad seasons and the bank, the bloody bank, I lost it; the lot, even the crop in the ground.

JIMMY: [*drunker*] Yeah, fuckin' gubmet. Fucks everybody up; everybody, eh? Eh? You allowed to walk down the street after sundown? Eh?

FRANK: Yeah, don't see why not.

JIMMY: Well I'm not. None of us are; you know we're not allowed in town, not allowed to go down the soak, not allowed to march…?

He mimes handcuffs and gaol by first putting his wrists together and then placing a hand downwards over his forehead with the fingers spread over his eyes.

Manatj grab us like that. Bastards…

FRANK: Who?

GRAN: Politjmans.

JIMMY: They can shoot our dawgs, anytime they want to. Bastards. They shot Streak. [*To* SAM *and* MILLY] Eh, you 'member Streak. Kill and show dawg, used to catch meat for every blackfella in Northam and they shot him. [*Miming*] Just like that. [*Maudlin, almost in tears*] Ay, Mill, he's married; got three kids and a wife.

MILLY: [*sympathetically*] *Nyorn, winyarn.*

GRAN: [*to* FRANK] Where they now?

FRANK: When we walked off I sent 'em to Perth, stayin' with her parents.

JIMMY *drags a wallet out of* FRANK'*s pocket.*

JIMMY: Show 'em that photo. Go on, mate, show 'em.

JIMMY *gives* FRANK *the wallet and stands.*

[*Wandering off*] Go on, show 'em.

SAM: Where you goin'?

JIMMY: I'm gonna strain the spuds.

FRANK *takes out the photo and passes it around.*

MILLY: All girls, eh?

GRAN: *Nyorn, winyarn,* pretty *koolangah* too.

SAM: Nice lookin' *yorgah.*

CISSIE: She come from Lake Yealering?

FRANK: No, met her at a dancin' contest; Charleston, at the Lux, in Perth.

SAM: How long since you seen your kids?

FRANK: Six months; haven't even sent 'em any money.

>   JIMMY *returns and falls over the bike in the dark.*

JIMMY: Oh, Jesus, me bloody leg! Fuck that bike!

>   JIMMY *kicks at the bike savagely.*

DAVID: Oh, Uncle Jimmy, don't do that; I just fixed it up.

JOE: [*jumping up*] Eh, *kongi,* David's been workin' on it all day. *Kienya.*

>   *He runs to rescue the bike, but collects an accidental blow from* JIMMY.

Ow! Me nose!

>   SAM *jumps up, runs to* JIMMY *and pushes him.*

SAM: You cut that out, you hear me?

JIMMY: You git!

>   *He swings an ineffectual punch at* SAM.

SAM: Just stop it, awright?

>   JIMMY *attacks and they engage in a ragged brawl. After a moment they separate and circle one another.* JIMMY *takes his coat off.*

JIMMY: Awright, come on, come on.

SAM: Stop it, you hear me? And none of your bitin'.

FRANK: I'd better go, Mrs Millimurra.

MILLY: Yeah, awright.

>   FRANK *stands.*

FRANK: And thanks for the really nice meal.

MILLY: That's all right. Eh! Cut it out, you two.

FRANK: Tooroo!

FRANK *leaves.* JIMMY *and* SAM *are locked together, cursing each other.* CISSIE *and* DAVID *rescue the bike from under their feet.* JOE *blows his nose and looks for blood on his sleeve.*

GRAN: Don't you hit him, Sam.

SAM: I will if he bites me.

GRAN: I'll stop you two fellas.

She charges at them, grabbing both by the hair and pulling viciously. They separate and she falls on her backside. MILLY *laughs.*

MILLY: Aw, Mum, you're cruel.

JOE *goes and tries to pick her up.* SAM *seizes his chance and sits on* JIMMY, *who thrashes about helplessly.*

JOE: Granny, git up, you're getting dirt all over you.

GRAN *gets up with help from* JOE.

JIMMY: Who do you think you are, fuckin' Jack Johnston?

SAM: You think you're fuckin' Jack Dempsey.

GRAN: I'll stop youse, I'll stop youse.

She takes her wahna stick and gives them both a solid poke in the ribs. They separate and get up, reluctantly.

[*To* SAM] Now git off him. You know he's *weern koort minditj.*

SAM: He ain't sick in the chest, he's sick in the bloody head.

JIMMY *crawls for his coat, then for the bottle.* MILLY *beats him to it.*

MILLY: This is real fightin' stuff, eh? Real fightin' stuff.

She pours it onto the ground. JIMMY *sits, head between his knees, and groans.*

SCENE FOUR

The Police Station and lock-up, Northam, night. Two separate cells imprison JIMMY *and* SAM. *The* SERGEANT *and* CONSTABLE *put possessions into drawstring bags and record their contents. Beside them stands a bottle of port, nearly empty.*

SERGEANT: Munday, James Emmanuel.

CONSTABLE: One mouth organ, one length of binder twine; tobacco tin, Wild Woodbine; one book, *Lasseter's Last Ride*, eightpence halfpenny.

SERGEANT: [*inspecting the bottle*] Port. Who got it for 'em?

CONSTABLE: [*laughing*] They're not sayin'.

JIMMY *takes out a mouth organ and plays 'Home, Sweet Home'.*

SERGEANT: Be that bloke camped down the goods yard. I'll check with publicans and pick him up in the morning...

[*Nodding at* JIMMY] Thought you took that thing off him.

CONSTABLE: [*picking up a bag*] I did, it's here.

SERGEANT: Musta had two of 'em. Get it off him.

The CONSTABLE *walks down to* JIMMY*'s cell*

CONSTABLE: Give me that instrument.

JIMMY: This ain't a hinstrument, it's a mouth organ.

CONSTABLE: Hand it over.

JIMMY: You already got one.

CONSTABLE: Give it here.

JIMMY: I gave you me other one.

CONSTABLE: Just bloody-well hand it over.

SAM: Give it to him, *gnoolya, baal nooniny barminy.*

JIMMY *relents and pokes it through the door. The* CONSTABLE *returns and puts it in the bag.*

JIMMY: Bastard.

CONSTABLE: Two mouth organs. Wish I knew how to play one of these.

JIMMY *picks up the toilet bucket.*

JIMMY: [*calling*] Eh, Sergeant! Sergeant!

SERGEANT: [*to the* CONSTABLE] See what he wants.

The CONSTABLE *walks to the cellblock doorway.*

JIMMY: [*calling*] Sergeant!

CONSTABLE: What do you want?

JIMMY: Tell your boss the *koomp* bucket's got a hole in it.

CONSTABLE: [*to the* SERGEANT] He reckons the piss bucket's got a hole in it.

SERGEANT: Bullshit; he can't aim straight.

CONSTABLE: There's nothing wrong with it, you not aimin' straight.

The CONSTABLE *returns to the bench.*

JIMMY: [*calling*] I'm aiming straight, all right. I'm a good shot. I can knock a rabbit's eye out at a hundred yards, and I *could* blow the sergeant's head off with a three-oh-three at six hundred, bloody oath.

SAM: Eh, *gnoolya, dubakieny.*

SERGEANT: Listen, Munday, if you know what's good for you, you'll shut up.

JIMMY: Him, he don't care. He's happy he's got us here. Fuck 'em! Fuck 'em! Fuck 'em all!

He hurls the bucket against the wall.

SAM: *Gnoolya,* you flamin' idiot.

SERGEANT: [*to the* CONSTABLE] That's government property. Stop him.

The CONSTABLE *goes to* JIMMY*'s cell carrying a baton.*

CONSTABLE: Put that down!

SAM: Stop it, *gnoolya,* steady down, steady down!

JIMMY *puts the bucket down and turns around as if to urinate in it. The* CONSTABLE *returns to the bench.*

SERGEANT: Damage to government property, to whit, one shit bucket. Add it to the charge sheet.

The CONSTABLE *gets out the charge sheet. Silence.*

JIMMY: [*calling*] I don't give two hoots of a lamb's tail. Never mind, Serge, I'll sing you a song. I'll sing you a hymn, if you like. [*Singing*]
    'Hail, Queen of Heaven, the ocean star,
    Guide of the wanderer here below,
    Thrown on life's surge, we claim thy care:
    Save us from peril and from woe.
    Mother of Christ, star of the sea,
    Pray for the wanderer, pray for—'
[*He stops abruptly.*]
No hymns. No good to you, you're a proper *mummari.* Proper *mummari,* fuckin' both of youse. [*Singing*]
    'When its springtime in the Rockies,
    I'm comin' back to you…'

SERGEANT: I think I preferred the mouth organ.

SAM: See you gettin' six months tomorrow, *gnoolya*.

JIMMY: [*calling*] Six months! I can do that on me fuckin' head.

SERGEANT: I'll see what we can do.

JIMMY: [*calling*] Yeah, you would. [*Singing*]
> 'Mammy, Mammy,
> How I love you, How I love you,
> My dear old Mammy…'

SERGEANT: Oh, gawd!

JIMMY: [*singing*]
> 'I'd walk a million miles
> For one of your smiles,
> My Ma-a-a-ammy.'

[*Calling*] Hey Serge, Serge.

SERGEANT: [*to the* CONSTABLE] Ignore him.

JIMMY: [*calling*] I seen that talkin' picture at the Palace, sittin' right up the front, the roped off section for blackfellas. Al Jolson makin' out he was black, poor white bastard.

SAM: Eh, *dubakieny*, *wahnginy*.

JIMMY: [*calling*] Sergeant! Sergeant!

CONSTABLE: [*to the* SERGEANT] Jesus, I wish he'd shut up.

JIMMY: [*calling*] Eh, Sergeant! You bin, you bin out to Gubment Well and told Mum and Milly me and Sam in here?… Eh? No, you wouldn't think of that.

SERGEANT: [*standing, to the* CONSTABLE] I'll leave you to it. I'm going to interview a few publicans.

CONSTABLE: Had enough?

The SERGEANT *exits towards the main street.*

JIMMY: [*calling*] Fuck you, you white bastard, fuck you. [*Singing feebly*]
> 'I don't give a damn for any damn man,
> That don't give a damn for me.'

SCENE FIVE

The courthouse at Northam, morning. The SERGEANT *stands near the* JP, *a local cocky, who sits at the bench.*

JP: What have we got?

SERGEANT: Not much.

JP: Good, I'm in a hurry.

SERGEANT: Two natives. One supplying.

JP: All right, let's get moving. I've got to get to a bank auction in Wongamine; tryin' to pick up a cheap binder.

SERGEANT: [*calling*] Francis James Brown.

> FRANK *enters and goes to the dock. The* SERGEANT *passes the* JP *a paper bag. The* JP *pulls the port bottle out of it and looks at it curiously.*

Evidence

> *The JP examines it and sniffs it.*

JP: Are Munday and, ah, what's-his-name, natives within the meaning of the Aborigines Act?

SERGENT: Yes, sir.

JP: What do you plead?

FRANK: Guilty with an explanation, sir.

JP: If you're guilty I can't see much point in an explanation.

FRANK: I'd still like to say something, sir.

SERGEANT: The accused has been warned on two previous occasions about associating with natives.

JP: All right, make it brief.

FRANK: I arrived in Northam a few days ago, and I was broke and I didn't have anything to eat for two days and I ran into Jimmy in the park and he—

JP: [*interrupting, to the* SERGEANT] Who?

SERGEANT: James Munday. He was one of the natives arrested along with the accused.

JP: [*to* FRANK] All right, get on with it.

FRANK: Well, he was a real mate to me. He took me to his home and gave me a meal of—

JP: [*interrupting, to the* SERGEANT] His what?

SERGEANT: His camp at Government Well.

FRANK: He gave me a meal of—

JP: [*interrupting*] Look, I'm not interested in what you had for dinner. If you've got an explanation, just tell me what it is.

FRANK: [*nervously*] And he even lent me a razor; I hadn't had a shave in several days. He and his family were very kind to me and when

he asked me to pick up a bottle of wine for him, I felt obliged to do
it.

JP: Were you aware that you were breaking the law?

FRANK: Yes sir, but I didn't—

JP: [*interrupting*] Is there any previous record?

SERGEANT: No.

FRANK: I've never been in trouble before. I am an ex-serviceman and I
settled at Lake Yealering.

JP: All right, I don't need your life story. I understand the difficulty
of the situation you were in, but it's my duty to protect natives
and half-castes from alcohol. In view of this, I sentence you to six
weeks imprisonment with hard labour.

> FRANK *steps down.*

SERGEANT: [*calling*] Samuel Nathaniel Millimurra and James Emanuel
Munday.

> *Pause. No one appears.*

[*Calling*] Samuel Nathaniel Millimurra and James Emanuel
Munday.

> *The* JP *looks at his fob watch.* SAM *enters alone.*

JP: [*to the* SERGEANT] Where's the other one?

SERGEANT: Don't know. [*Yelling*] James Emanuel Munday. Come on,
Jimmy. Get a move on.

> JIMMY *enters, tying a bit of binder twine around his trousers,
and stands next to* SAM.

JP: I hope you're not making a mockery of the court by delaying
proceedings.

JIMMY: Sorry, sir, I was on the shit bucket… toilet… Got a guts ache,
sir.

> SAM *nudges him.*

SERGEANT: The two accused were apprehended in Bernard Park
yesterday at approximately nine-twenty p.m. They were both
under the influence of liquor. Munday was in possession of one
bottle of wine, three parts empty. [*Indicating*] That is the bottle
there, sir. Upon being placed in separate cells, Munday became
noisy and abusive. At one stage he damaged a toilet bucket. He

threatened me and used indecent language. He threatened to 'blow my head off.'

JIMMY: I did not.

SERGEANT: Silence in the court.

JIMMY: [*to the* JP] What I said was that if I had a—

SERGEANT: [*interrupting*] Silence!

JIMMY: [*to the* JP] But he's telling it wrong. What I said was, that—

JP: [*interrupting*] Order, order. Now you be quiet, Munday, you'll get your chance shortly.

JIMMY: But all I was gunna say was that what—

JP: [*interrupting*] Shut up, you bloody idiot, or I'll charge you with contempt of court.

SAM: Yes, sir.

JP: [*indicating* JIMMY] Not you, him. [*To the* SERGEANT] Are there any previous records?

SERGEANT: Munday has several previous convictions for the same offence and one of unlawful disposal of government rations.

JP: And Millimurra?

SERGEANT: One, drinking, when in the company of Munday.

JP: Are they related?

SAM: He's my *gnoolya*, sir.

JP: He's your what?

SERGEANT: They're brothers-in-law. Millimurra's married to—

JP: [*interrupting*] All right. I see this is your sixth offence related to alcohol. On the last occasion you were sentenced to fourteen days imprisonment. This time your sentence is three months imprisonment with hard labour.

He stands.

All right...

SERGEANT: What about Millimurra, sir?

JP: Ah, fine of twenty-five shillings. Any costs?

SERGEANT: Two and sixpence.

JP: And two and six costs, in default seven days imprisonment.

SERGEANT: He'll need time to pay.

JP: All right, fourteen days. Stand down.

The JP *hurries out.*

SCENE SIX

Government well, Northam, early morning. It is winter, GRAN *builds a fire.* SAM *carries water and* DAVID *gets ready for school.* CISSIE *huddles near the fire, wrapped in a blanket.* MILLY *fries fat in a camp oven.*

MILLY: Cissie, I want you to write that letter to Uncle Jimmy 'fore you go.

SAM: What's to eat?

CISSIE: Oh, Mumma.

MILLY: [*to* SAM] Damper there, dip in the camp oven.

SAM: Me *gnoolya*'s better off than I am, bet he's not eating bread 'n fat for breakfast.

GRAN: Joe be back directly with a *wilbra*.

DAVID: [*to* CISSIE] You want to hurry up. I ain't waitin' for you.

> CISSIE *doesn't move.* JOE *appears, wet and dejected, with empty rabbit traps.*

GRAN: Rabbits *wah*?

JOE: Open. These ain't worth settin'. Bloody rabbits only look at 'em and they snap off.

SAM: Well, grab a bit of breakfast, I want you to help me cut the rest of them posts today.

> JOE *eats damper and dip.* GRAN *gives him a cup of tea.*

MILLY: Cissie, come on, hurry up.

CISSIE: [*weakly*] Mum, I feel worse.

> *She coughs.* DAVID *stuffs a piece of damper in his pocket and grabs his bike.*

MILLY: You wait for your sister.

DAVID: Come on, Cissie.

GRAN: What's wrong with you?

MILLY: What's the matter, you *minditj*?

> *She feels* CISSIE*'s forehead.* CISSIE *coughs and her mother rubs her back. They all gather around her with increasing concern.*

God, she's burnin' up.

CISSIE: [*holding her throat*] Hurts, Mum, here; hurts when I cough.

MILLY: Well, no school for you today, my girl. [*To* SAM] You ain't goin' post cuttin' today, and David, you walk to school.

DAVID: Aw, Mum!

MILLY: Don't, 'Aw Mum' me. Joe, you git on that bike and go and ask Uncle Herbie for a lend of his horse and cart. We takin' her to the doctor straight away.

JOE *takes the bike from* DAVID.

SAM: Aw Mill, can't you and Mum take her? I only want another hundred posts and I'll have enough *boondah* to pay me fine.

GRAN *grabs* JOE *before he rides off.*

GRAN: Ask him for some *gnummarri* for me.

MILLY: You can go this afternoon.

JOE: Okay, Gran.

SAM: What doctor you takin' her to?

DAVID *gets on the bike behind* JOE *and they ride off together towards the main street.*

GRAN: More better take her straight to the hospital.

SAM: [*calling after* JOE *and* DAVID] We'll wait down the road for you.

JOE: Okay!

JOE *and* DAVID *exit.*

MILLY: [*to* SAM] You better ask Skinny for a couple of dozen bags.

SAM: He'll want me to cut an extra one hundred and fifty posts for that.

MILLY: Well, cut 'em then, and get a lend of some bag needles and don't forget binder twine.

SAM: Another twenty posts.

MILLY: You an' Joe can patch up the sides, then go down the dump an' see if you can find more tin for the roof. Bloody place is colder than the North Pole. And that old baldy had better cough up with some more blankets.

SAM: Come on girlie, I'll carry you.

SAM *picks up* CISSIE *and they all leave. The dogs bark.*

SCENE SEVEN

The Police Station, Northam, winter's morning, 1932. SERGEANT CARROL *walks into the station and sits down to read the local newspaper, the Northam Advertiser. Outside the Chief Protector's office,* JIMMY *waits around.* MR NEVILLE *briskly approaches his office.*

JIMMY: Mr Neville, Mr Neville! I wanna see you.

NEVILLE: The office opens at nine o'clock.

JIMMY: Can't wait, gotta train to catch.

NEVILLE: The native's entrance is around the back.

JIMMY: I'm not waitin 'round there all day.

NEVILLE: [*affronted*] I beg your pardon?

JIMMY: I only wanna train fare to Northam.

NEVILLE: You can wait around the back and you'll be attended to in due course.

JIMMY: I'm not sittin' down there all bloody day.

NEVILLE: What's your name?

JIMMY: Jimmy Munday.

NEVILLE: Munday, Northam… Oh yes, I've got a good fat file of police reports on you. What are you doing in Perth?

JIMMY: Mindin' me own bloody business.

NEVILLE: Munday, let me give you a piece of advice: sugar catches more flies than vinegar.

> NEVILLE *storms into his office, sits at his desk, and starts to read his mail as* CONSTABLE KERR *limps into the police station.*

SERGEANT: Afternoon.

CONSTABLE: Sorry, had to walk, got a crook leg playin' footy.

SERGEANT: When was that?

CONSTABLE: Sat'dy… You were there.

SERGEANT: It's all right, I just wasn't sure whether you were on the field.

> MISS DUNN *arrives at the office.*

JIMMY: Missus! Hey, Missus!

MISS DUNN: Good morning.

JIMMY: Missus, I wanna see Mr Neville.

MISS DUNN: I'm not sure if he's in yet.

JIMMY: He's in there, all right. I seen 'im, an asked 'im for a train fare.

MISS DUNN: And what did he say?

JIMMY: Sometin' about catchin' flies.

MISS DUNN: All right, I'll mention it to him. There's a bench on the back verandah, if you'd like to wait there.

> MISS DUNN *enters the office.*

SERGEANT: [*to the* CONSTABLE] Oh yeah, you rated a mention in the '*Tiser*.

CONSTABLE: I know.

MISS DUNN: [*seating herself*] Good morning, Mr Neville.

NEVILLE: Morning, Miss Dunn.

MISS DUNN: There's a native outside, wants to see you about a train fare.

NEVILLE: [*abruptly*] I know. He can wait.

> NEVILLE *continues to read as* JIMMY *ambles around the back of the office and sits on the waiting bench.* MISS DUNN *opens the rest of the mail.*

SERGEANT: [*reading*] 'Towards the end of the first quarter, Kerr marked in front of goal... but kicked out of bounds. Towns eight: twenty-two; seventy points to Federals ten: twelve; seventy-two points.'

CONSTABLE: I know the score.

> SERGEANT CARROL *continues reading and chuckles to himself.* NEVILLE *lays an open letter on the desk in front of him.*

NEVILLE: Miss Dunn, would you mind getting Sergeant Carrol in Northam on the line?

> MISS DUNN *picks up the phone and dials.*

SERGEANT: [*to the* CONSTABLE] And you got another mention.

MISS DUNN: [*into the receiver*] Hello, operator; Northam nine please... Thankyou.

SERGEANT: [*reading*] 'In front of goal, Gillet put Kerr in possession who... kicked out of bounds...' Sea breeze in, was it?

> JIMMY *ventures into* MISS DUNN*'s part of the office.*

JIMMY: S'cuse me, Missus.

CONSTABLE: [*to the* SERGEANT] I kicked a couple of goals.

JIMMY: [*to* MISS DUNN] I wanna see him.

MISS DUNN: All right, what's your name?

JIMMY: Jimmy Munday. I wanna train fare; mixed goods leaves at eleven o'clock.

MISS DUNN: All right, I'll ask him...

She goes to NEVILLE's *desk.*

That native, Jimmy Munday, is waiting to see you. He wants a train fare.

NEVILLE: Well, he'll just have to wait.

MISS DUNN: [*returning to her desk*] I'm afraid he's very busy at the moment.

The phone rings in Northam.

He'll see you later on.

The CONSTABLE *answers the phone.*

CONSTABLE: }   Hello, Northam Police... Yes.
JIMMY: } [*together*]   [*to*MISSDUNN]Look,Missus.Ijust got outa gaol an' I wanna train fare back home.

The phone rings in the Chief Protector's Office.

CONSTABLE: [*to the* SERGEANT] Niggers' Department.

The SERGEANT *takes the phone.*

MISS DUNN: [*to* NEVILLE] He says he's just been released from gaol. [*Into the receiver*] Hello, Aborigines Department.

NEVILLE: Then he should have the price of a train fare.

MISS DUNN: [*into the receiver*] Yes, hold the line please. [*To* NEVILLE] Northam.

SERGEANT: Hello.

NEVILLE: [*to* MISS DUNN] Oh, he can have a travel voucher if he comes back after two.

He picks up the phone. MISS DUNN *hangs up and relays* NEVILLE's *message to* JIMMY.

SERGEANT: Hello.

NEVILLE: Sergeant Carrol... Neville. Sergeant, we seem to be running into problems again. I've received correspondence from the Town Clerk to the effect that they are opposing the gazetting of the Guilford Road site as a native reserve. They consider it unsuitable.

SERGEANT: It's got a water supply and a couple acres of grazing land.

> MILLY *and* GRAN *approach the police station.*

NEVILLE: Apparently the Council has plans to develop it.

SERGEANT: What as?

NEVILLE: [*reading*] As a 'recreation park, for boy scouts and picnic parties'.

SERGEANT: Pretty recent plans.

GRAN: [*shouting*] Chergeant! Chergeant!

SERGEANT: [*to the* CONSTABLE] For Christ's sake, see who that is.

NEVILLE: Sorry, Sergeant.

SERGEANT: Between you and me and the gatepost, the Council'd prefer it if you sent 'em to Moore River or somewhere.

GRAN: Chergeant!

> *The* CONSTABLE *goes to the door.*

NEVILLE: Most councils would prefer that, Sergeant, but the place is bursting at the seams.

GRAN: [*to the* CONSTABLE] I wanna see him.

CONSTABLE: He's on the phone.

NEVILLE: You can only do your best, but I'm afraid you'll have to come up with another alternative.

CONSTABLE: [*to* GRAN] You'll have to come back later on.

GRAN: You ain't the boss… Chergeant!

NEVILLE: I'll be in touch soon.

SERGEANT: 'Bye, Mr Neville.

CONSTABLE: [*to* GRAN] I don't want any lip from you.

NEVILLE: Better leave you to it.

> NEVILLE *and the* SERGEANT *hang up.*

GRAN: [*to the* CONSTABLE] And I don't want any from you. [*To the* SERGEANT, *shouting*] Hey, Chergeant, your man gettin' cheeky out 'ere.

SERGEANT: [*to the* CONSTABLE] For God's sake, let 'em in.

MILLY: *Choo, choo.* Mum, don't shout.

SERGEANT: They can be heard all the way down the bloody street…

> *They enter.* JIMMY *barges into the Chief Protector's Office.*

JIMMY: Mr Neville.

NEVILLE: I thought you were told to wait outside.

JIMMY: I only want a train fare.

NEVILLE: I distinctly heard Miss Dunn tell you to come back after two.

JIMMY: Too late, mixed goods leaves at eleven.

NEVILLE: You can catch the Kalgoorlie train at five.

JIMMY: I don't want to go to Kalgoorlie.

SERGEANT: [*to* GRAN *and* MILLY, *taking out the ration book*] Why weren't youse here yesterday?

NEVILLE: [*to* JIMMY, *exploding*] Wait outside, then.

GRAN: [*to the* SERGEANT] Had to go t'ospital.

NEVILLE: A travel voucher please, Miss Dunn.

MILLY: [*to the* SERGEANT] My gel's sick in 'ospital.

> JIMMY *ambles out and stretches out on the bench.*

SERGEANT: [*taking out packets of rations*] Sugar, tea.

MILLY: We need blankets.

SERGEANT: [*to the* CONSTABLE] See if you can find some bi-carb. There. Here's your stick of nigger twist, Gran.

MILLY: What about blankets?

SERGEANT: [*taking out a packet*] Flour... What?

MILLY: Blankets. My girl's in 'ospital with 'monia and pleurisy.

GRAN: An' we want blankets.

SERGEANT: Sorry, blankets not here yet, Milly.

GRAN: Her name Mrs Millimurra. Proper church married, New Norcia, white dress an' all.

MILLY: Got paper to prove it, and birth 'tificate.

GRAN: [*at the approaching* CONSTABLE] Not like some people, I bet.

CONSTABLE: Here's your bi-carb.

GRAN: What about them *wanbru*?

CONSTABLE: What?

MILLY: Blankets!

SERGEANT: Look, there's nothin' I can do about it except put in a reminder to the Department in Perth. Why don't youse go around to St John's and ask the vicar?

MILLY: For blankets? He'll give us nothin', he's like that.

GRAN: [*adopting a praying attitude*] Yeah, when he come to Gubment Well he goes like that with his eyes closed and he says the Lord will help you, and now he prays with his eyes open, 'cause time 'fore last Wow Wow bit him on the leg... musta wanted a bit a' holy meat.

MILLY: You forgot our meat order.

SERGEANT: No meat this week.

MILLY: What?

SERGEANT: Finished; in future no meat is included in rations.

GRAN: Why?

CONSTABLE: There's a bloody depression on.

MILLY: What are we gunna do for meat?

CONSTABLE: There's plenty of roos and rabbits.

GRAN: What about *tjirrung*?

CONSTABLE: What about what?

MILLY: Fat!

SERGEANT: Fat is classified as meat. I'll see what I can do about the blankets for youse.

MILLY: I want 'em 'fore Cissie gits outa hospital.

SERGEANT: I can't promise anything, but I'll check with the Department.

GRAN: An' you're supposed to be native 'tector.

> GRAN *and* MILLY *take their rations and exit.*

SERGEANT: Looks like I'm the one needs protectin'.

CONSTABLE: Should put a pinch of strychnine in the flour.

SERGEANT: Too late to adopt the Tasmanian solution.

NEVILLE: [*yelling*] Munday!

> JIMMY *stands and enters the office.*

The eleven o'clock mixed goods, make sure you're on it.

> *He hands* JIMMY *the voucher.*

And try to keep out of trouble for a while.

> JIMMY *shuffles off at a snail's pace.*

You'd better get a move on if you're going to catch that train.

JIMMY: Don't think I'll worry about the mixed goods, catch the five o'clock Kalgoorlie train instead. Haven't been down in the big smoke for a few weeks, might have a bit of a look around.

NEVILLE: You get on that train—

JIMMY: [*interrupting*] You know one thing about Fremantle Gaol? Even some of them screws are polite—not like this place. [*Walking off*] Native Protector, couldn't protect my dog from fleas.

NEVILLE: [*returning to his office*] Cheeky, too bloody cheeky.

SCENE EIGHT

Government Well, day. JIMMY *is mending a pair of shoes.* GRAN *and* MILLY *sew bags together.* SAM *enters with buckets of water and sits down, exhausted.* JOE *enters with a sugar bag slung over his back.*

JIMMY: There y'are, Joe, good as new.

JOE: *Woolah! Moorditj!*

JIMMY: Learnt me trade well, in Freo.

MILLY: [*to* JOE] What did you get?

JOE: Fat, taters, onions.

SAM: You get meat?

MILLY: No *boondah* for meat.

JIMMY: Wish I'd known the meat ration was cut out when I saw Mr bloody Neville the other day.

GRAN: He take no notice of you.

JOE: Cissie ready to come home from hospital.

MILLY: How do you know?

JOE: Sergeant told me. Saw him at the Post Office.

SAM: When, today?

JOE: She's waiting there now.

MILLY: Why didn't you ask him to give youse a lift 'ome?

JOE: Him? Hah!

JIMMY: Only time blackfellas git a ride off him is when he's takin' you to gaol.

MILLY: Well, she ain't walkin' home, anyways. Sam, you better get a lend of Herbie's cart.

JOE: It's got the wheel broke, Mum.

MILLY: Then you'll have to get a lend of old Skinny Martin's.

SAM: Another hundred posts, I bet.

MILLY: Ne'mine the posts, long as we git her home.

JIMMY: Yeah, go and ask him, *gnoolya*, and I'll solve the meat problem at the same time.

MILLY: What you talkin' about?

JOE: Yeah, *kongi*, I know where his wethers runnin'.

JIMMY: Him, I know that bastard's farm like the back a me hand.

JOE: Old Skinny might be bony but his sheep are cruel fat.

GRAN: You wanna watch out. Chergeant catch you, he give you six months just like that.

JIMMY: Oh, bugger old baldy.

> JOE *takes a knife and starts to sharpen it.*

JOE: *Woolah*, sheep guts and lo-o-o-vely hot damper.

GRAN: Don't git *tjeuripiny*, you ain't got the horse and cart yet.

SAM: Don't worry 'bout that, Mother-In-Law, as long as he reckons he's gettin' somethin' for nothin' he'll be in it, *kwonna tjuellara*.

JOE: Come on, let's get goin', I'm hungry.

JIMMY: Well, he ain't gitten it for nothin' this time.

SAM: Better bring Wow Wow, help round the sheeps up.

GRAN: Put them shoes on, Joe.

JOE: Don't need no dawg. Don't need no shoes either, Granny, I can run better barefoot and faster than Wow Wow.

JIMMY: Come on, *Gnoolya*, we'll git one of the skinny old bastard's sheep and bring it home on his own cart.

MILLY: Me and Mum, we'll wait for youse in the park, all right?

GRAN: Youse be careful now, you hear me?

MILLY: Come on, Gran.

JIMMY: [*miming slitting the sheep's throat*] *Mirri*-up, *mirri*-up. *Allewah koorkantjerri gnuny nooniny dininy, woort dininy.*

SCENE NINE

The Chief Protector of Aborigines' Office, Perth, day. MISS DUNN *types while* MR NEVILLE *dictates from a list of warrants.* SERGEANT CARROL *approaches.*

NEVILLE: Munday, Herbert Williams and wife Wooleen. Munday, James Emanuel. Munday, May Alice. Millimurra, Samuel… wife Millicent and three children: Joseph, Cecilia and David.

> *There is a knock on the door.* MISS DUNN *rises to answer it.*

SERGEANT: Sergeant Carrol, Northam. I'm meant to be seeing—

NEVILLE: Sergeant, I wasn't expecting you until later. Train on time?

SERGEANT: [*entering*] Not exactly, sir, I caught the seven-twenty mixed goods.

NEVILLE: When are you returning? Come through, sit down.

> *They sit at* NEVILLE'*s desk.*

SERGEANT: On the five-fifteen Kalgoorlie train.

NEVILLE: Right, I don't want to delay you, so we'll deal with the matter in hand. Miss Dunn, would you bring the Northam file, please, and the warrants?

> MISS DUNN *locates the file, collects the warrants and brings them to* NEVILLE.

Sergeant, as I mentioned on the phone, Doctor Aberdeen examined the natives camped at Government Well.

He goes through the file and finds the doctor's report.

And found them to be... 'rotten with scabies', and as a result of— ah, well, various submissions, it's been decided to transfer the entire native population to the Moore River Settlement.

SERGEANT: Yes sir. We can give up looking for a site for a new reserve, then.

NEVILLE: The transfer is a temporary measure, Sergeant. Well, I've got all the warrants, following your own census, Sergeant; a total of eighty-nine natives.

He hands over the warrants.

If that list changes at all, let me know and I'll obtain any additional warrants. It's essential that the town and shire are quite devoid of natives after the seventeenth.

SERGEANT: Yes, sir.

NEVILLE: I've arranged with the railway authorities for an AR coach and brake van to be at your disposal on the seven-twenty a.m. train on the seventeenth. It will arrive, I am assured, at ten-twenty-nine a.m. at Midland and I've arranged for the Midland Railway Company to attach both to a train to leave immediately for Mogumber. Should arrive at three p.m. You'll be met and proceed on foot to a quarantine camp at Long Pool, just east of the settlement. [*Handing him an order form*] I've authorised expenditure of one and sixpence per native for food en route to be purchased in Northam, and for buckets of tea to be available at Chidlows and Muchea. Following your recommendation, Sergeant, no native will need to leave the train at any stage of the journey. I'll leave it to your discretion what personal luggage is to accompany your charges, preferably as little as possible.

SERGEANT: What about conveyances? There's a couple of sulkies and a spring cart.

NEVILLE: I'm afraid if they don't fit in the brake van they don't go.

SERGEANT: What about horses and dogs?

NEVILLE: They certainly can't go. You'll have to make arrangements to store the property and look after the livestock left behind.

SERGEANT: How long is that likely to be?

NEVILLE: Well, your guess is as good as mine. Until the scabies are cleared up and a new reserve is gazetted.

SERGEANT: Or until after the election.

NEVILLE: I wouldn't know about that.

SERGEANT: They won't leave their dogs behind.

NEVILLE: No, but the superintendent won't have any dogs coming with them to the settlement.

SERGEANT: What about a small road party to go with the conveyances and horses?

NEVILLE: Personally, I'd prefer to see them go in one operation.

SERGEANT: One officer could handle it, and it would avoid a lot of problems at my end, sir.

NEVILLE: All right, you're in the front line. But I want as many as possible on the train, and definitely no dogs.

SERGEANT: No, I'll attend to the dogs when I clean up the camp.

NEVILLE: [*standing*] Good, I don't need to impress upon you the absolute confidentiality of the matter.

SERGEANT: Yes, sir.

NEVILLE: Well, I won't keep you. You've got a couple of hours before your train.

SERGEANT: Yes, I'm going down to Boan's to pick a few presents for the Mrs and the kids.

NEVILLE: Good, thank you for your co-operation. And don't forget, no dogs.

SERGEANT: [*standing*] Thank you, Mr Neville. All the best for Christmas.

NEVILLE: And to you and yours.

The SERGEANT *moves past* MISS DUNN*'s desk.*

MISS DUNN: Goodbye, Sergeant. Have a happy Christmas.

SERGEANT: Same to you, madam.

The SERGEANT *exits.*

SCENE TEN

Government Well, Northam, day. CISSIE *with the aid of a knife is looking for lice in* DAVID'*s hair.* MILLY *and* GRAN *sew. A car approaches.*

CISSIE: Keep still!

DAVID: Well stop diggin' a hole in me head.

CISSIE: Hold still, I got a big one.

GRAN: [*looking up at the car*] *Gneean nitja koorling?*

MILLY: *Allewah, manatj!*

CISSIE: They got Dad and Joe and Uncle Jimmy.

MILLY: Gawd, hope they haven't been caught stealin' a sheep.

> *Everyone is silent. The three men are escorted to the camp by the* SERGEANT *and* CONSTABLE.

What's up?

JIMMY: [*nodding at the* SERGEANT] Just listen to him.

SAM: We're all goin'.

> *He gestures Nyoongah fashion as the* CONSTABLE *goes through a pile of warrants.*

SERGEANT: Millimurra and Munday.

GRAN: Goin'? Where?

SERGEANT: I've got warrants here for the arrest and apprehension of all of youse.

MILLY: What for? We ain't done nothin'.

SERGEANT: I never said you did. You're bein' transferred, every native in Northam's goin'!

MILLY: Goin' where?!

SAM: Mogumber.

CONSTABLE: You're being transferred to the Moore River Native Settlement.

GRAN: I ain't goin'.

CONSTABLE: You're all goin'. You're under arrest.

GRAN: What for? We done nothin' wrong.

SERGEANT: It's for health reasons. Epidemic of skin disease.

JIMMY: Bullshit, I'll tell you why we're goin'.

CONSTABLE: You wouldn't know.

JIMMY: You reckon blackfellas are bloody mugs. Whole town knows why we're goin'. 'Coz *wetjalas* in this town don't want us 'ere, don't want

our kids at the school, with their kids, and old Jimmy Mitchell's tight
'coz they reckon Bert 'Awke's gonna give him a hidin' in the election.

CONSTABLE: What the hell would you know? You don't even vote.

JIMMY: I know more about *wetjala*'s gubment than you do, and what
I'm tellin' you's the truth.

CONSTABLE: Bullshit.

SERGEANT: Shut up, will you? I don't know whose idea it is, it's got
nothin' to do with me.

CONSTABLE: You barkin' up the wrong tree, Munday.

JIMMY: Bullshit, Jimmy Mitchell's—

SERGEANT: [*interrupting*] Look, I know this much; Jimmy Mitchell's
got nothin' against blackfellas, or anybody else, for that matter.

JIMMY: No, he's got nothin' against 'em. Not worth losin' a bloody
election over, that's all. I'll tell youse somethin': you're wastin'
your fuckin' time.

CONSTABLE: Hey, all right.

JIMMY: 'Coz *wetjalas* aren't gonna vote for 'im. You know why? 'Coz
he's got all them Chinamens workin' on his farm at Grass Valley
and *wetjalas* don't like that. He's gunna get rida the blackfellas, he
should get rid of them Chinamens too.

SERGEANT: Oh, Jesus, shut up will youse? You're all goin'and that's
that, an' if you don't co-operate you'll just go along for resisting
arrest and escaping legal custody.

SAM: When are we supposed to be leavin'?

SERGEANT: On the seven-twenty mixed goods train in the morning.
You'll be camping in the goods shed overnight.

MILLY: What about all our things?

SERGEANT: You can pack personal things belonging to you. Herbert
Munday is too old to go by road, Sam and his family will be going
on the road party, with his horse and spring cart. Jimmy and Gran
can go on the train.

GRAN: I ain't goin' on no train, I'm goin' with Sam and Milly. You're
not makin' me go on no train.

CONSTABLE: You'll get pretty hot walkin'.

SERGEANT: Listen, Granny, the road trip will take four days. You'll be
better off on the train.

GRAN: Chergeant, I ain't goin' on no train. You can put me in gaol if
you want to.

She begins to wail and cry.

I'm not goin' by train; what we leaving Gubment Well for? *Wetjala warrah, warrahmut, oooh*!

SERGEANT: All right, all right, Gran, you can go by road if you want to.

GRAN: [*recovering instantly*] I am, too.

CONSTABLE: It's her funeral if she doesn't make it.

JIMMY: It'll be your funeral.

SERGEANT: That's enough. Jimmy, you're comin' with us. The rest of you better start packin' and go and get Herbie's horse and cart.

SAM: What about our kangaroo dogs?

SERGEANT: I'm under strict orders that no dogs are allowed to go.

SAM: What, leave the dogs behind?

JIMMY: Come off it, Sergeant, how are they gonna get meat on the way?

CONSTABLE: You won't need to worry, you'll be on the train.

SERGEANT: There's plenty of rabbits.

JOE: What, are you gonna run 'em down?

SERGEANT: According to Dr Aberdeen you've got a serious heart condition, so you'll be going on the train, Jimmy.

JIMMY: I'm not goin' on no fuckin' train.

GRAN: Chergeant, I'm not leavin' Wow Wow behind. If I can't take him, I'm not goin'.

MILLY: Who's gonna look after our dogs?

CONSTABLE: We'll attend to them.

MILLY: Yeah, we know that.

JIMMY: With a police bullet.

GRAN: [*frantically*] You're not gonna shoot Wow, you're not gonna shoot Wow Wow. You hear me, Chergeant? I'm not goin'.

> GRAN *is frantic now. She tears her hair and throws plates and mugs about.*

SERGEANT: Oh Jesus, take your bloody mangy Wow Wow, whatever you call it. Take the bloody lot, just remember to be ready to move out tomorrow morning.

> *The police escort* JIMMY *away. The family looks on in stunned silence.* CISSIE *clings to her mother and cries.*

END OF ACT ONE

Neville (James Beattie) gives Jimmy (Ernie Dingo) his train voucher as Miss Dunn (Annie O'Shannessy) looks on. Photo by Garry Summerfield.

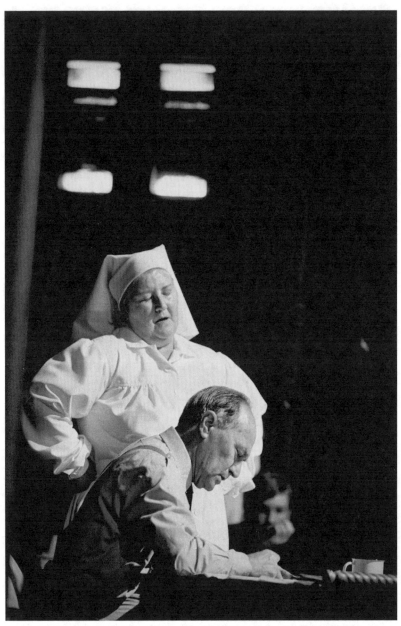

Doreen Warburton and Ben Gabriel as Matron and Mr Neal in the W.A. Theatre Company production. Photo by Tony McDonough.

ACT TWO, MOORE RIVER

SCENE ONE

The track to Moore River, day. The family enters. They are laden with possessions, hot, dusty and tired. In a clearing at the Long Pool Camp, Moore River Native Settlement, JIMMY *erects a bush shade over a tent. The family is approached by a tracker,* BILLY KIMBERLEY. *He smokes a clay pipe and carries a whip.*

BILLY: Mornin', mornin'.

SAM: Gawd, who the fuckin' hell are you?

BILLY: I'm a politjman, name Billy Kimberley.

DAVID: [*amazed, to* CISSIE] He's a policeman!

SAM: More like Tom Mix.

> BILLY *holds out his pipe.*

BILLY: You got *killarla*?

CISSIE: He might be Buck Jones.

SAM: Ain't got none.

GRAN: You ain't politjman, you just black tracker.

BILLY: All right, you fella follow me, now. I show you where your camp. Come on now, this way.

> *They follow* BILLY *towards the clearing.*

CISSIE: [*to* DAVID, *nodding at* BILLY] Gawd, he's black.

DAVID: He ain't black, he's purple!

GRAN: *Choo*, you fellas want to *dubakieny wahnginy*. He might be *boolyaduk*.

JOE: Ah, Granny, he's *yuart*. [*Making an open gesture*] He's like that.

> *They approach* JIMMY.

JIMMY: 'Ullo! 'Ullo! How's everybody?

SAM: Tired, bloody tired.

> *They start to unload their possessions.*

BILLY: Now, you fellas sit down along this place, you hear me? Matron comin' bye and bye.

MILLY: Who?

JIMMY: Matron, Superintendent's Missus. She runs the hospital.

MILLY: When's she comin'?

BILLY: Dunno, 'morrow, must be next day. She comin' you fella all
wait this place now.

    BILLY *exits.*

JOE: Gawd strewth!

    The children laugh at the departed BILLY.

JIMMY: Anyway, how you, Mill? Joe and you kids? Mum?

MILLY: We're all right, I s'pose.

JIMMY: And how you, Mother?

GRAN: I'm *warrah, gnuny tjenna minditj*; and I got no *gnumrnarri.*

JIMMY: Never mind, Mother, here.

    JIMMY *takes some tobacco from his pocket and gives it to her.*

GRAN: *Winjar kaep?*

JIMMY: Straight down the pad, there.

MILLY: You kids get a billy each and go and get some water.

DAVID: Oh boy, I'm gonna have a swim.

MILLY: No, you ain't. Might be *bilbarl, dugaitj*, anything down there.

DAVID: Aw, Mum.

MILLY: I said no!

JOE: I'll come with youse.

MILLY: All right, you can if Joe's with youse.

DAVID: Come on, Cissie!

MILLY: Take the water bag.

    They take it and run off.

JIMMY: Kimberley tell youse where to get the tucker tonight?

MILLY: No.

JIMMY: Down the kitchen.

SAM: Where?

JIMMY: Soup Kitchen.

SAM: Good tucker?

JIMMY: More like three-course bloody pig swill. Treacle and bread or
bread and fat, take your pick.

SAM: What about *daitj*?

JIMMY: Meat? You gotta be jokin'.

MILLY: What about a sheet of iron for the fireplace?

JIMMY: Don't worry, I know where I can get one. Come on, Sam, I'll knock it off, you can watch.

> JIMMY *exits, followed by* SAM.

GRAN: *Cooo, cooo!* You come back now, Jimmy, you hear? *Cooo!*

> MILLY *unrolls a blanket. She and* GRAN *are left alone.*

MILLY: Come on, Mum, lay down and have a rest.

SCENE TWO

A clearing near the Moore River, day. JOE, DAVID *and* CISSIE *fill a water bag from billy cans.*

JOE: Don't spill it.

CISSIE: I'm tryin' not to.

> DAVID *tries the water.*

JOE: Good *kaep.*

CISSIE: Don't spit in it.

DAVID: I ain't.

> *Unseen, two girls approach:* TOPSY *and* MARY, *who carries a bag of meat.* DAVID *takes his shirt off.*

Where we gonna swim?

CISSIE: Dunno, let's find a place.

> DAVID *sees the girls.*

DAVID: *Tjinung, yorgahs!*

> *They all look.*

JOE: Gidday.

MARY: Hello.

TOPSY: You fellas amongst the Northam lot?

JOE: Yeah, that's Cissie, and that's David. I'm Joe, Joe Millimurra. We're all Millimurras.

TOPSY: I'm Topsy, that's Mary. She's from up North.

JOE: They grow 'em pretty up there.

> DAVID, CISSIE *and* TOPSY *giggle.*

What you got in the bag?

TOPSY: *Yonga*, we're takin' it up to Uncle Herbie.

CISSIE: Uncle Herbie's our uncle too.

JOE: How come he's your uncle?

TOPSY: His cousin is our grandfather—I think, on our mum's side. How come he's your uncle?

CISSIE: He's married to our aunt. You know, not really married.

> *She and* DAVID *dissolve into the giggles.*

JOE: [*to* MARY] Are you related too?

MARY: No.

> DAVID *and* CISSIE *laugh.*

DAVID: Eh, *gnoon*, you're cruel!

JOE: Shut up. Take the water back, you two.

DAVID: What about our swim?

JOE: I'll take youse later, get goin'!

> CISSIE *and* DAVID *run off, shouting:*

CISSIE and DAVID: [*together*] Joe's got a girlfriend, Joe's got a girlfriend.

> *They exit.*

TOPSY: I got to get goin' to set the tables for supper.

> TOPSY *exits.*

JOE: [*to* MARY] I can take the meat for you if you like.

> MARY *approaches with the bag of meat.*

What's your name?

MARY: Mary.

JOE: I know that. Your full name?

MARY: Mary Dargurru.

> *She runs after* TOPSY, *still carrying the meat.*

JOE: Mary!

MARY: [*stopping*] Yeah?

JOE: The *daitj*.

MARY: Oh, yeah.

She returns to him with it.

JOE: [*taking the meat*] When will I see you again?
MARY: Dunno.
JOE: Can you be here tomorrow?
MARY: I'll try.
JOE: Don't say 'try', say you will be.
MARY: All right.
JOE: Same time.
MARY: I'll try, I mean, yes.
JOE: I'm glad we're not related.
MARY: So am I.

She runs off. JOE *watches her into the distance.*

SCENE THREE

Long Pool Camp, Moore River, a hot day. CISSIE *and* DAVID *play knuckle bones.* MILLY *and* JOE *enter with water.* GRAN *sits in the shade. The dogs bark.* BILLY *trudges on, followed at a distance by* MATRON NEAL, TOPSY *and* MARY.

BILLY: [*calling*] You fella got them *doothoo* tied up?
SAM: [*calling*] Yeah.
BILLY: Come on, Missus, come on.
SAM: [*to* JOE] Nothin' to bite on him, he's all skin and bone.
JOE: Plenty of meat on the matron.
BILLY: You fella stand up straight, now.
DAVID: Hey, that's them girls.
BILLY: [*poking his whip at* DAVID] You shut up now.
JOE: Hey, old man, *dubakieny*.
MATRON: Good morning, good morning. Now, all the family here?
GRAN: My boy Jimmy ain't.
MATRON: [*checking her list*] Munday, James Emanuel. Oh, yes, with
    the train party. It's all right, we've seen him. Now let's see. Samuel,
    Millicent, Joseph, David and Cecilia, and the grandmother. Good.
    Now I'm the matron, Matron Neal, and I'm in charge of the hospital
    and Topsy here is helping me.
DAVID: We already seen her.
JOE: Shut up, *gnoon*.

MATRON: Now, seeing you came here for health reasons, I'd just like to examine you.

GRAN: What for?

MATRON: For any skin complaints, Granny.

GRAN: Scabies? We ain't got it.

SAM: Even the dogs ain't got it.

BILLY: You be quiet now, Matron make you no more sick fella.

JOE: What's he yakkin' about? We ain't sick.

BILLY threatens JOE nervously with the whip.

MATRON: All right, Billy. Now David, you first. Come on.

He doesn't move. BILLY prods him with the whip.

Billy!

DAVID: I ain't takin' me pants off.

JOE: Me either.

TOPSY giggles.

MATRON: Just your shirt will do for a start.

She begins to take DAVID's shirt off. TOPSY moves to help him but he jumps away and does it himself.

DAVID: Git!

MILLY: David.

MATRON examines his hands, elbows and knees, ankles and abdomen.

MATRON: Good boy. Now you, Cecilia.

She checks her much the same way.

MILLY: None of us got it.

MATRON checks her and SAM.

MATRON: No, they're a healthy lot, a credit to you, Millicent. All right Joe, take your shirt off.

JOE: There's nothin' wrong with me.

MATRON: No, I'm sure there's not. I just want to check.

She checks him in the same way.

How old are you, Joe?

JOE: Dunno.

MILLY: He's seventeen next burnin' season.

MATRON: He's a strapping lad.

GRAN *gets up.*

No need to get up, Gran, I'm sure you're all right.

GRAN: Joe, show Matron your belly button, go on.

She pulls JOE's *shirt up.*

What do you think of that, Matron?

JOE: Aw Gran, *kienya.*

GRAN: Isn't that the neatest belly button you seen? Have a look, Matron. I brought him into the world with me own two hands.

SAM: [*laughing*] Mumma!

MATRON: You did a very good job, Granny.

GRAN: I brought plenty *kooloongah* into this world, Matron.

MATRON: Well, there doesn't seem to be anything wrong with your family, Millicent. I won't bother putting you on the sulphur, but I want you all to use the washing facilities every day before every meal and after you've been to the toilet. Now, look at those fingernails, David; perhaps you could set an example by going off and scrubbing them.

DAVID *exits reluctantly.*

Well, Milly, here are a few more cakes of Lysol soap and some handkerchiefs for the children. Well, busy, busy, Topsy, one more family visit. 'Bye for the present. Goodbye, Gran.

She goes to leave, then stops.

Oh, how many dogs have you got in the camp?

They look at each other in silence, then:

SAM: A couple of kangaroo dogs, and Granny's dog.

MATRON *strides off, followed by* BILLY, *who stops her some distance away.*

BILLY: They got that many, missus.

He holds up seven fingers.

JOE, DAVID and CISSIE: *Wahrdung, wahrdung,* black crow!

MATRON *exits.* BILLY *glares at the children.*

SCENE FOUR

Moore River Native settlement, a clearing in the pine plantation, night.
JOE *creeps on and lets out a mopoke call. Pause. He calls again, and*
the call is returned. MARY *approaches, carrying a crumpled parcel.*

JOE: You got here all right.
MARY: I brought you a present.

> *She hands him the crumpled parcel and they sit on a log.*

JOE: What is it?
MARY: Damper, oven cooked, mixed with emu fat and they're real raisins, not weevils.

> *They giggle and eat.*

JOE: You comfortable? Sit closer. How long you been here?
MARY: About five minutes.
JOE: I know that, I mean how long you been here at the settlement?
MARY: This was my third Christmas… I wish I was back home. I hate this place, I hate everything in it.
JOE: Even me?
MARY: No, I don't hate you.
JOE: Them *wetjalas* treat you all right?
MARY: *Gudeeahs*? Matron and Sister Eileen are all right. They try to be nice, but I don't like Mr Neal. He scares me.
JOE: He don't scare me.
MARY: I don't like the way he looks at me.
JOE: Well, you got me now, for what I'm worth.

> *He laughs.*

MARY: He's always hangin' around where the girls are workin'; in the cookhouse, in the sewin' room. And he's always carryin' that cat-o'-nine tails and he'll use it, too.
JOE: Bastard, better not use it on you or any of my lot.
MARY: He reckoned he was gunna belt me once.
JOE: What for?
MARY: 'Coz I said I wasn't gunna go and work for *guddeeah* on a farm.
JOE: Why not? Be better than this place.
MARY: No! [*With shame*] Some of them *guddeeahs* real bad. My friend went last Christmas and then she came back *boodjarri*. She reckons

the boss's sons used to belt her up and, you know, force her. Then they kicked her out. And when she had that baby them trackers choked it dead and buried it in the pine plantation.

JOE: What? You dinkum?

MARY: That's true.

JOE: [*stunned*] The bastards. The fuckin' bastards.

> MARY *starts to cry.*

Come on, Mary, stop that. You know somethin'?

MARY: What?

JOE: I don't like you.

> *She draws away.*

I love you.

> *They embrace.*

MARY: I have to go back, Matron will find out.

JOE: Stay a bit longer.

> *She kisses him.*

MARY: I have to go now, or she won't let me out again.

JOE: When will I see you again?

MARY: Tomorrow.

JOE: Same time?

MARY: Yeah.

JOE: Same log?

MARY: Yeah. Joe, I don't like you either.

> *They laugh and embrace.* MARY *runs away.* JOE *watches after her.*

SCENE FIVE

The Moore River Settlement, a hot morning. JIMMY *ambles about outside the Superintendent's office.* MR NEAL *approaches. He has a hangover.*

NEAL: Hey, you, you're with the Northam lot, aren't you? What are you doing here?

JIMMY: What's it look like I'm doing?

NEAL: You're supposed to be up in the quarantine camp.

JIMMY: Quarantine camp, me arse.

NEAL: You're out of bounds and you know it.

JIMMY: Come off it, you know that quarantine camp is a load of bullshit, so don't try and tip it over me.

NEAL: I'll attend to you later.

He heads for his office.

JIMMY: You know, if fertiliser was in short supply you'd make a bloody fortune.

He sniggers.

NEAL: [*mumbling*] Another bloody troublemaker.

He sits at his desk. MARY *brings him tea on a tray. He leers at her body.* MATRON *enters, almost catching him.*

MATRON: Where did you get to yesterday?

NEAL: You know very well I had to go to Moora to see about—

MATRON: [*interrupting*] To spend the day in the hotel drinking. Don't imagine no one sees you come in, the condition you were in—fine example.

NEAL: I've got to get away from the place now and again.

MATRON: What about me? I was at the quarantine camp from dawn till dusk again yesterday.

NEAL: Done them all?

MATRON: Yes, eventually.

NEAL: How many have got it?

MATRON: Scabies? Mrs Mason and her three youngsters.

NEAL: Yes.

MATRON: That's all, just the four of them. I've isolated them, put them on sulphur and regular bathing.

NEAL: Four of 'em, only cases of skin disease? Only four?

MATRON: Yes, Alf. I can recognise a case of scabies when I see one.

NEAL: And you've examined the lot of them?

MATRON: Yes, I haven't been going up the Long Pool for a picnic.

NEAL: Are you telling me out of eighty-nine dumped on me, only four of them have got the bloody disease?

She puts the record book in front of him.

Good God, woman, what's the bloody game? Eighty-nine natives in a bloody quarantine camp I've just busted me gut to get ready on time, and there's nothing bloody well wrong with 'em?

MATRON: Alf, there's no need to lose your temper and no need for bad language. They should be cleared up in a few days.

NEAL: The whole job's a waste of time. They could have been treated in Northam.

MATRON: The only health hazard in the camp are the dogs.

NEAL: What dogs?

MATRON: There's about fifty of them, and a good many in less than healthy condition.

NEAL: How did the dogs get here?

MATRON: With the road party, apparently.

NEAL: No one told me anything about dogs.

MATRON: One per family.

> *She exits.*

NEAL: That's one too many. [*Calling*] Billy! Billy!

> *He unlocks the armoury cupboard and gets a rifle and ammunition.*

BILLY: [*off*] Yeah, comin' boss.

> NEAL *counts out the ammunition.* BILLY *enters.*

Yeah, Boss?

NEAL: Get the horses and a length of rope, Billy.

BILLY: Yeah, boss.

> NEAL *takes a rifle and ammunition. They exit.*

SCENE SIX

A clearing in the pine plantation. Moore River Native Settlement, night. A camp fire burns. JIMMY *and* SAM *are painted for a corroboree.* JIMMY *mixes wilgi in tobacco tin lids, while* SAM *separates inji sticks from clapsticks.* JOE *arrives with an armful of firewood and pokes at the fire.*

JOE: They comin' now.

BILLY: [*off*] Get no rain this place summertime.

> BILLY *and* BLUEY *enter and remove their shirts.*

JIMMY: Eh? Where you fellas been?

BLUEY: Aw, we been pushing truck for Mr Neal.

BILLY: He goin' Mogumber.

BLUEY: [*miming taking a drink*] Doin' this fella.

JOE: He'll be *minditj* tomorrow.

> BLUEY *and* BILLY *paint themselves with wilgi.*

BILLY: My word you fellas pr-retty fellas.

BLUEY: *Wee-ah*, plenty *wilgi*.

BILLY: Eh? You know my country, must be walk two, three days for this much. Your country got plenty.

> JIMMY *strikes up a rhythm on the clapsticks.* BLUEY *joins him.*

JIMMY: [*singing*]

> Tjinnung nitjakoorliny?
> Karra, karra, karra, karra,
> Moyambat a-nyinaliny a-nyinaliny,
> Baal nitja koorliny moyambat a-moyambat moyambat,
> Moyambat nitja koorliny moyambat.
> Kalkanna yirra nyinny kalkanna,
> Yirra nyinniny, yirra nyinniny,
> Moyambat a-kalkanna moyambat a-kilkanna
> Yirra nyinniny, yirra nyinniny, yirra nyinniny,
> Karra koorliny kalkanna karra karra koorliny kalkanna.
> Karra koorliny, karra koorliny, karra koorliny,
> Woolah!

BLUEY: Eh, what that one?

JIMMY: That's my grandfather song. [*Miming with his hands*] He singin' for the *karra*, you know, crabs, to come up the river and for the fish to jump up high so he can catch them in the fish traps.

SAM: [*pointing to* BILLY*'s body paint*] Eh! Eh! Old man, what's that one?

BILLY: This one *bungarra*, an' he lookin' for berry bush. But he know that fella eagle watchin' him and he know that fella is cunnin' fella. He watchin' and lookin' for that eagle, that way, this way, that way, this way.

> *He rolls over a log, disappearing almost magically.* BLUEY *plays the didgeridoo and* BILLY *appears some distance away by turning quickly so the firelight reveals his painted body. He dances around, then seems to disappear suddenly. He rolls back over the log and drops down, seated by the fire.*

BLUEY, SAM and JIMMY: *Yokki! Moorditj! Woolah!*
JIMMY: Eh? That one dance come from your country?
BILLY: Nah. That one come from that way, lo-o-ong way. *Wanmulla* country. Proper bad fellas.
SAM: Well, I won't be goin' there.
JOE: Me either!

> JIMMY, JOE *and* SAM *laugh.* SAM *jumps to his feet with the clapsticks.*

SAM: This one *yahllarah!* Everybody! *Yahllarah!*

> *He starts a rhythm on the clapsticks.* BLUEY *plays didgeridoo.* JIMMY, *and then* JOE, *join him dancing.*

Come on! Come on!

> *He picks up inji sticks. The Nyoongahs,* SAM, JIMMY *and* JOE, *dance with them.* BILLY *joins in. They dance with increasing speed and energy, stamping their feet, whirling in front of the fire, their bodies appearing and disappearing as the paint catches the firelight. The dance becomes faster and more frantic until finally* SAM *lets out a yell and they collapse, dropping back to their positions around the fire.* JIMMY *coughs and pants painfully.*

[*To* JIMMY] Eh! Eh! [*Indicating his heart*] You wanta *dubakieny*, you know your *koort minditj.*
BILLY: This country got plenty good dance, eh?
BLUEY: *Wee-ah!*
JIMMY: Ah, *yuart*, not too many left now. Nearly all finish.
BILLY: No, no, no. You song man, you fella dance men. This still your country. [*Flinging his arms wide*] You, you, you, you listen! *Gudeeah* make 'em fences, windmill, make 'em road for motor car, big house, cut 'em down trees. Still your country! Not like my country, finish… finish.

> *He sits in silence. They watch him intently.* JOE *puts wood on the fire. He speaks slowly.*

BILLY: *Kuliyah.* [*Miming pulling a trigger, grunting*] *Gudeeah* bin kill 'em. Finish, kill 'em. Big mob, 1926, kill 'em big mob my country.

> *Long pause.*

SAM: *Nietjuk?*

BILLY: I bin stop Liveringa station and my brother, he bin run from Oombulgarri. [*Holding up four fingers*] That many days. Night time too. He bin tell me 'bout them *gudeeah*. They bin two, three stockman *gudeeah*. Bin stop along that place, Juada Station, and this one *gudeeah* Midja George, he was ridin' and he come to this river and he see these two old womans, *koories*, there in the water hole. He says, what you doin' here? They say they gettin' *gugja*.

He mimes pulling lily roots and eating.

Midja George say, where the mans? They over by that tree sleepin', and Midja George, he get off his horse, and he bin belt that old man with the stockwhip. He bin flog 'em, flog 'em, till that *gudeeah*, he get tired. Then he break the bottle glass spear, and he break the *chubel* spear.

He grunts and mimes this.

And that old man, he was bleedin', bleedin' from the eyes, and he get up and he pick up that one *chubel* spear, and he spear that one *Midja George*.

He demonstrates violently.

And that *gudeeah*, he get on his horse, he go little bit way and he fall off... finish... dead.

JIMMY: Serve the bastard right.

BILLY: No, no, no bad for my mob. Real bad. That old man and his two *koories*, they do this next day.

He indicates running away.

Two *gudeeah* come looking for Midja George. They bin find him dead.

Silence.

[*Holding up a hand*] Must be that many day. Big mob *gudeeah*. Big mob politjmans, and big mob from stations, and shoot 'em everybody mens, *koories*, little *yumbah*.

He grunts and mimes pulling a trigger.

They chuck 'em on a big fire, chuck 'em in river.

They sit in silence, mesmerized and shocked by BILLY*'s gruesome story.*

JIMMY: Anybody left, your mob?

BILLY: Not many, gid away, hide. But no one stop that place now, they all go 'nother country.

JOE: Why?

BILLY: You go there, night time you hear 'em. I bin bring cattle that way for Wyndham Meat Works. I hear 'em. Mothers cryin' and babies cryin', screamin'. *Waiwai! Wawai! Wawai!*

They sit in silence staring at BILLY *who stares into the fire. Suddenly a night hawk screeches.*

SAM: Gawd, I'm getting out of here.

JIMMY: Me too!

BLUEY: Hm, hm, hm, hm, *wee-ah, wee-ah*!

They quickly pick up their things and leave. JOE *remains alone.*

SAM: You comin'?

JOE: Go on, I'll catch you up. Go on!

JIMMY: You watch out.

He pinches his throat with thumb and forefinger.

JOE: I'll be all right.

SAM: Don't forget the *kaal*.

JOE: Okay.

They exit. JOE *looks around, pokes the fire, stands and waits. The moon begins to rise. There is a low mopoke call. He replies with a similar call and gets a reply.* MARY *runs into the clearing. They embrace.*

I didn't think you were gunna get here.

MARY: I bin watchin' youse for nearly half an hour.

JOE: *Kienya!*

MARY: I mean listenin', not watchin'.

JOE: It's all right, wasn't man's business. Did you have any trouble gettin' away?

MARY: Nah. Topsy's coverin' up for me. I'll just walk in the dinin' room in the mornin'. They won't miss me.

JOE: [*nervously*] Where you gunna sleep tonight?

They kiss. MARY *withdraws from him and sits on the log.*

She begins to cry. He checks that they are alone and sits close beside her on the log.

JOE: Eh? What's up? Come on, tell me what's up. You been fightin' with someone?

She shakes her head.

Come on! Tell me what's the matter.

MARY: Mr Neal.

JOE: Yeah, what about him?

MARY: He's tryin' to make me go and work at the hospital.

JOE: Well, what's wrong with that?

MARY: Everything.

JOE: You get better tucker.

MARY: It's more than that, Joe.

JOE: What d'ya mean?

MARY: When Mr Neal sends a girl to work at the hospital, it usually means...

JOE: Means what?

MARY: That he want's that girl... for himself.

JOE: *What?*

MARY: Everyone know, even the *wetjalas*.

JOE: Rotten, stinkin', lowdown bastard. I'll kill him!

MARY: Joe...

JOE: I'll smash his head in with a *doak*!

MARY: Joe, listen!

JOE: Filthy pig. You not goin' anywhere near that hospital!

MARY: If I don't, he reckons he'll send me back home.

JOE: Home? Where?

MARY: Wyndham. He reckons he send me up home 'coz I'm a give girl.

JOE: Like hell you are.

MARY: I don't want to go up there to marry no old man.

JOE: You're meant to be gettin' married to me.

MARY: Mr Neal not gonna let us get married.

JOE: [*exploding*] Jesus! [*Indicating running*] We're doin' this tonight, right this fuckin' minute.

MARY: Joe, you'll get in big trouble!

JOE: I'll get in bigger trouble if I have to chip that walrus-faced bastard. I'll kill him.

MARY: Joe, listen! Where we gunna go?

JOE: Home, Northam.

MARY: What about your mum and dad?

JOE: We'll tell 'em now, come on, come on.

MARY *just stands there.*

Come on. I'm gunna show you my country. Got a big river, swans, beautiful white swans.

JOE *picks up his shirt and a billy of water, which he tips on the fire. He leads* MARY *off into the darkness.*

SCENE SEVEN

Long Pool Camp, Moore River, night. Dogs bark. JOE *and* MARY *appear as shapes in the darkness.* JOE *tries to quieten the dogs. He approaches the tent.*

JOE: Mum, Dad? You wake?

He looks back at MARY, *who stands alone.*

Mum, Dad!

MILLY: Hmm, who is it?

JOE: It's only me.

MILLY: It's Joe.

The tent lights up as a match is struck and a hurricane lamp lit.

SAM: What's he want?

He crawls out.

Where you bin? We been home for hours.

MILLY *appears behind him.*

JOE: Mary's with me.

MILLY *takes the lamp and goes to* MARY.

MILLY: Mary! You should be in the compound.

JOE: She ain't goin' back there.

JIMMY *appears, sleepy and dazed.*

JIMMY: What's goin' on?

JOE: It's only me, *kongi!*

MILLY: She can't stay here, Joe, she's a compound girl.

JOE: I know, Mum, we're runnin' away—tonight!

SAM: Now? What for?

JOE: 'Cause Neal's givin' Mary a bad time.

SAM: Can't be all that bad.

JOE: Neal's after her for himself. He's tryin' to make her work in the hospital and he keeps sayin' he's gonna send her back to her lot to marry some old man—and he won't give no permission for us to get married.

MILLY: [*comforting* MARY] There's gotta be some other way than clearin' out.

JOE: Only other way's to stiffen that bastard in the dark.

He goes to MARY.

MILLY: They'll catch you sooner or later, son, and you'll go to gaol.

JIMMY: That right, neph, you clear out. Gaol's *yuart*, only a *wetjala* thing. Don't worry about it.

MILLY: No, I'll do the worryin'.

SAM: Where's Granny?

MILLY: She's stoppin' with Aunty Wooleen.

She picks up a camp oven and breaks damper and crams it into a billy.

There's a bit of *merrang*, it's all we got.

She gives it to MARY. SAM *gives* JOE *a blanket. He begins to roll it.*

Where will you go?

JOE: [*smiling*] Northam. I'm gonna show Mary the swans. Well, 'bye Dad, Uncle Jimmy! Say goodbye to Gran.

He moves towards the tent. His mother stops him.

MILLY: Don't wake the kids. Less they know the better.

JOE: [*kissing her*] Bye, Mum.

MARY *kisses* MILLY, *then she and* JOE *walk away swiftly. They look back and wave, then vanish into the darkness.* MILLY *cries quietly.*

JIMMY: [*calling after them*] You can jump the rattler 'bout half a mile outside a' Mogumber. Keep to the gravel country. Trackers won't find your tracks.

SCENE EIGHT

The Superintendant's Office, Moore River Native Settlement, day.
MR NEAL *is sitting at his desk reading the* West Australian, *10 April 1933. The headlines read, 'Government Routed', 'Three Ministers Defeated', 'Labor Majority of Ten', 'Premier Loses Northam Seat', 'Two To One For Secession'.* MATRON *enters.*

MATRON: I've got some news for you.

NEAL: I know. I've read it, a bloody massacre.

> MATRON *is pleased, almost gloating.*

Premier's gone in Northam... Looks like a majority of about ten... A bloody Labor Government.

MATRON: That's the good news... Two natives appear to—

NEAL: [*interrupting*] The only good news is the referendum: two to one.

MATRON: Beg your pardon, but I thought you might—

NEAL: [*interrupting*] The bloody secession referendum. In favour, one hundred and sixty three thousand six hundred and fifty three, against seventy thousand seven hundred and six.

> *He stands and walks to the door, thrusting the paper at* MATRON.

MATRON: Where are you going?

NEAL: Moora.

MATRON: What, holding a wake?

NEAL: I'm not staying here to listen to you gloat all bloody day.

MATRON: Well, before you go off to commiserate with your cronies in the hotel, you'd better do something about the runaways.

NEAL: What bloody runaways?

MATRON: [*looking him in the eye*] Mary Dargurru, and Joe Millimurra.

NEAL: Since when?

JIMMY: Mary wasn't in the dormitory last night, or at breakfast this morning.

NEAL: Jesus, they'll be miles away. Why didn't you say something last night?

MATRON: I thought she might have been somewhere else.

NEAL: [*yelling*] Billy!

MATRON: Apparently you told her she was going to work at the hospital and stay in the nurses' quarters.

NEAL: Who told you that? [*Yelling*] Billy!

BILLY: [*off*] Comin', boss.

MATRON: It seems she was terrified at the prospect of working in the hospital.

NEAL: They're all scared of the dead.

MATRON: I think she was scared of the living.

> BILLY *enters, buttoning up his jacket.*

NEAL: Two runaways, Billy! You know Joe Millimurra, Northam native?

BILLY: Yeah, boss.

NEAL: And Mary Dargurru?

BILLY: That one Dargurru, my countryman. [*Pointing with his chin*] She got go back Oombulgarri.

NEAL: You better get movin'! They'll be at the railway line by now.

BILLY: Ne'mine boss. I find 'em. Take 'em whip?

NEAL: Yes, take your whip, and pick up some tucker from the store. Here!

> *He throws a stick of tobacco onto the floor.* BILLY *picks it up.*

BILLY: Thanks, boss.

> BILLY *exits.* MATRON *turns to follow him.*

MATRON: As matron in charge of the hospital, I thought it was my job to allocate nursing aides.

NEAL: I was only trying to help you.

MATRON: Or yourself.

> *She exits.* NEAL *collapses into his chair.*

SCENE TEN

A clearing near the railway line at Mooloombeeni, early morning. MARY *is curled up asleep under a blanket.* JOE *appears with a billy can of water and his hat full of quandongs. He gently wakes* MARY. *She wakes in fright.*

JOE: Look, quandongs.

MARY: Oooh, my feet still hurt.

JOE: Let's have a look.

> JOE *washes and rubs her feet. She flinches.*

They're a bit skinned. [*Nodding at the quandongs*] Eat 'em.

MARY: Oh, that feels good. [*She bites into a quandong.*] Aagh! They're sour!

JOE: They're nice with sugar on 'em.

> MARY *jumps up and begins to vomit.* JOE *supports her. A magpie warbles.*

You all right?

MARY: Gawd! Oh! I've never been sick like that in my life before.

> *She retches again.*

JOE: You'll be all right once we get on the rattler. We'll get a nice cosy truck.

> JOE *sits her down and puts a blanket around her. She rests against him and recovers. A magpie squawks and* JOE, *immediately on his guard, jumps up and grabs his doak.* BILLY KIMBERLEY *appears and rushes at him with a stockwhip in one hand and handcuffs in the other.* JOE *dodges him.* MARY *is sick again as* BILLY *advances slowly and menacingly on* JOE.

BILLY: You two fella, silly fella. Everyone run away. Wait here for the choo choo. [*Swinging the whip at* JOE]
Choo, choo, choo, choo.

> JOE *dodges the whip and threatens him with the doak.*

JOE: Go back, old man. I don't want to hurt you.

BILLY: [*pointing with his chin to* MARY] She got to come back, she my countryman.

> MARY *vomits.* BILLY *drops the handcuffs and the two men crouch and circle each other.*

JOE: She's comin' with me.

BILLY: She give girl. Mitjer Neal says she gotta come back.

JOE: Fuck Mr Neal!

BILLY: You bad boy, *Tjenna Guppi* gunna git you!

JOE: And fuck the *Tjenna Guppi* too!

JOE *grabs the end of the whip and wrenches it from* BILLY, *sending him tumbling forward.* JOE *leaps on him and twists the whip around his neck.* MARY *staggers across to them. The train whistle blows in the distance.*

MARY: Joe, Joe you choking him!
JOE: I'll kill the old bastard!
MARY: Get up off him. Please! Please, for my sake!
JOE: Gimme them handcuffs! Handcuffs, quick!

MARY *throws him the handcuffs.* JOE *handcuffs* BILLY'*s hands in front of him, releases the whip and throws it down. He starts to go through* BILLY'*s pockets.*

[*To* MARY] You run, run, ru–un flat out to the hill! I'll catch you up!

MARY *starts to pick up their possessions.*

Leave them! Just run… Run!

MARY *runs, hopping painfully on bruised and lacerated feet.* JOE *finds the keys to the handcuffs and throws them away. He picks up their gear.*

You shouldn't fight young fella, old man. Here, tucker.

JOE *thrusts quandongs into* BILLY'*s pockets, pushes his hat down over his head, and runs after* MARY.

BILLY: Thas awright, thas awright. *Gudeeah* politjman git you bye and bye, you see.

BILLY *picks up his whip with his handcuffed hands, pokes it in his belt and walks off slowly. The train thunders past.*

SCENE TEN

The Superintendent's Office, Moore River, day. BILLY, *still handcuffed, limps past the Long Pool Camp followed by* DAVID, CISSIE *and* TOPSY, *all shouting 'Black crow, black crow'.* MR NEAL *reads the paper at his desk as* BILLY *approaches.*

BILLY: Mitjer Neal, Mitjer Neal! Eh boss!
NEAL: Come in.

BILLY *enters.*

Jesus, what the bloody hell happened?!

BILLY: He bin chuck me off my 'orse and he bin knock me silly fella with a *waddi*.

MATRON *walks in briskly with an arm full of linen. She stops in her tracks when she sees* BILLY.

MATRON: Goodness me, what happened?

NEAL: Well, he never caught Millimurra, Millimurra caught him.

MATRON: [*putting the linen on* NEAL'*s desk*] Oh, you poor man, where's the keys?

NEAL: Listen, Billy, where did you catch up with them?

BILLY: I bin find 'em Moolambeenee.

NEAL: Where were they heading?

BILLY: And that fella bin say he gunna hang me from Christmas tree like that.

He demonstrates.

Eh boss, you bin take 'em off handcuffs now?

MATRON: Where are the keys?

NEAL: All right, which way did they go?

BILLY: They bin run along train line. Train comin', whoo, whoo!

NEAL: All right, which— way— was— the— train— going?

BILLY: Goin' along train line.

NEAL: I know that, you blithering stone-age idiot!

MATRON: [*pointing left and then right*] Billy, was the train going that way or that way?

BILLY: [*pointing with his chin to her left*] He bin go that way, *Kaggardu*.

NEAL: You bloody fool of a man! What did you let him jump the bloody train for?

BILLY: He bin knock me silly fella, with a big stone. [*Indicating his back and then ribs*] He bin kill 'em me here, here, and in the guts. Aw, he bad fella. [*Desperately, almost in tears*] Eh boss, you bin take 'em off handcuffs now?

NEAL: [*to* MATRON] Get the keys out of his pocket.

BILLY: No key, boss.

NEAL: Where are they?

MATRON *starts to find quandongs.*

BILLY: Dunno, boss... that one, he bin—

NEAL: [*interrupting*] You bloody incompetent savage. Where are the
    fuckin' keys?

BILLY: He bin chuck 'em away. He bad boy that one!

> MATRON *has a handful of quandongs but no keys.* NEAL *puts his
> hat on and prepares to leave.*

NEAL: Come on, looks like a blacksmith's job.

MATRON: Then you'd better send him down to the hospital. I'll examine
    him and give him some dinner.

> MATRON *looks at them and at the quandongs.*

BILLY: They good tucker, missus.

> *She laughs.*

NEAL: I can't see anything funny about this.

MATRON: I know you can't.

> NEAL *and* BILLY *walk off.* MATRON *bites on a quandong but it's
> bitterly sour. She picks up the linen and leaves.*

END OF ACT TWO

Monton Hansen as Sam. Photo by Tony McDonough.

ACT THREE, NORTHAM

SCENE ONE

Government Well Aboriginal Reserve, Northam, day. A few burnt out relics of the camp remain. JOE *and* MARY *stare about blankly.*

JOE: Grass ain't burnt.

MARY: What d'ya mean?

JOE: *Manatj*... [*Bitterly*] Burned everything, those bastards! [*He looks at the rubble.*] We camped just 'ere.

He leads MARY *to the spot.*

[*Pointing up and off*] See them rocks up there? Me and Cissie used to slide down them on pieces of tin when we was little. Magpies used to nest in that white gum tree.

MARY: Probably still do.

JOE: Yeah, s'pose so.

He sifts through the rubble and unearths a rabbit trap.

One a' Dad's.

He finds a wine bottle.

One of Uncle Jimmy's.

He puts it down carefully and continues the search.

MARY: Where did you get water?

JOE: Soak, down the creek.

MARY: Good *kaep*?

JOE: Sometimes. Mum used to always growl about it. She used to reckon it was harder than Uncle Jimmy's head. She'd be real upset if she saw the place now. Gran too. 'Specially Gran.

He sees something, off.

Oh, no!

He drags on the burnt remains of DAVID*'s bike.*

MARY: Whose was that?

JOE: Bastards! They reckon they was gunna look after everything we left behind.

MARY: Never mind, it's all over now.

JOE: It'll never be over!

He throws the bike down viciously.

MARY: Come on, *dubakieny.*

JOE *picks up a rabbit trap and inspects it. He is pleased with it and they walk off.*

SCENE TWO

A street in Northam, day. JOE *and* MARY *carry their swag, billy can and the rabbit trap.* SERGEANT CARROL *approaches.*

SERGEANT: Hey… You're one of the Millimurras, aren't you?… Joe?

JOE: Yeah.

SERGEANT: What are you doin' back in Northam?

JOE: We're livin' here.

SERGEANT: Who's this?

JOE: Me missus.

SERGEANT: Where are you staying?

JOE: Not at the Shamrock, that's for sure!

SERGEANT: You can't camp at Government Well.

JOE: What did you burn everything for?

SERGEANT: We're simply following orders.

JOE: What, to burn a push bike? I thought you were meant to look after our stuff till we come back.

SERGEANT: Look! I don't know nothing about no push bike.

JOE: What about rations?

SERGEANT: I can't help you there. Since all the natives have shifted out, Northam is no longer a ration depot.

JOE: We never shifted out, we was booted out. Anyway, what happened to the horses?

SERGEANT: They were in terrible nick. We had to shoot one, the other one's down at Martin's, I think.

JOE: Trust him to grab one.

SERGEANT: He didn't grab it, it just wandered onto his property.

MARY *grabs* JOE's *sleeve and tries to lead him away.*

MARY: Come on, Joe!

SERGEANT: Where's the rest of your lot? Not here, I hope.

JOE: You oughta know where they are, you dragged 'em there.

SERGEANT: All right, all right. Look, I don't care where they are so long as they're not here. Just make yourself scarce and don't go campin' anywhere you're not s'posed to be—and that includes Government Well.

JOE: Yeah, you made sure of that!

The policeman exits. JOE *watches him go.* MARY *tugs at him and they exit.*

SCENE THREE

Northam Police Station, day. SERGEANT CARROL *enters. At the Protector of Aborigines' Office, Perth,* MISS DUNN *steps in briskly and settles to typing.* SERGEANT CARROL *picks up the phone.*

SERGEANT: Hello. Hello, operator, a Perth number: B-M-nine-seven-oh-seven. Nine-seven-oh-seven. Yes, thanks Sybil, can't complain. Yourself?

He hangs up as MR NEVILLE *enters his office, carrying a briefcase.*

NEVILLE: Good morning, Miss Dunn. You're bright and early.

MISS DUNN: Good morning, Mr Neville. I thought I'd get a few pages of your Royal Commission submission typed before the telephone starts for the day.

Her telephone rings. She answers it.

Hello, Aborigines Department... yes... [*To* NEVILLE] It's Sergeant Carrol, Northam.

The phone rings in the police station. SERGEANT CARROL *answers it.*

NEVILLE: Thank you. Would you mind having a look at the mail when you have a moment?

NEVILLE *goes to his desk and takes the call.* MISS DUNN *hangs up.*

SERGEANT: Hello, Northam Police. Hello.

NEVILLE: Hello. Hello, Sergeant. Neville, Aborigines.

SERGEANT: Hello.

NEVILLE: Hello, Sergeant. Are you on the line?

SERGEANT: Hello, Mr Neville. It's a crook line.

NEVILLE: There's an appalling cracking noise, but I can hear you. Did you find out how many—

SERGEANT: [*interrupting*] As far as I can ascertain, the only natives here are Joe Millimurra and girl who he claims is his wife—Mary, I think. They're not actually camped in the town.

NEVILLE: Dargurru.

SERGEANT: Pardon?

NEVILLE: The girl. Mary Dargurru. Rhymes with kangaroo. D-A-R-G-U-double R-U.

The SERGEANT *fumbles for a pencil and writes on the desk.*

SERGEANT:... Double R, U. Yeah... Haven't had any bother with them. Millimurra's working at Lockyers, they're not collecting rations.

NEVILLE: Well, I've had two letters from the Town Clerk. The Council's still adamant that no natives remain in the Northam area.

SERGEANT: I know, I had a yarn with the Town Clerk last week; they're putting something into this Royal Commission, apparently.

NEVILLE: Well, you'd better apprehend them, anyway.

SERGEANT: What about warrants?

NEVILLE: Dargurru's a minor, and Millimurra's guilty of absconding with her: it carries a mandatory six months. You can hold him on the existing warrant; the girl can be sent down here under escort. I'll organise to have her met at Midland. Can you pick them up today?

SERGEANT: Yeah, I suppose so.

NEVILLE: Good, and let me know if any more natives return to the district. I've written to the Town Clerk letting him know that any Northam natives released from the settlement have undertaken not to return to the Northam District.

SERGEANT: Good-oh, Mr Neville.

NEVILLE: And let me know which train you're putting the girl on.

SERGEANT: Good-oh, sir.

NEVILLE: Thankyou, Sergeant.

They hang up as MISS DUNN *puts a thick pile of typing on* NEVILLE'*s desk.*

MISS DUNN: That's the section on settlements completed.

NEVILLE: [*taking a pile of notes from his briefcase*] Oh thankyou. Here's the next lot, keep you busy for a while. Did you get a chance to do the mail?

MISS DUNN: Yes; a couple of accounts and a letter from the Western Australian Historical Association.

NEVILLE: What do they want?

MISS DUNN: They'd like you to present a paper at their next meeting. Shall I write and tell them you're too busy at present?

NEVILLE: No, I'm very interested; I'll reply myself.

He begins drafting a reply while she commences typing. CONSTABLE KERR *enters the police station and begins to remove his hat and coat.*

SERGEANT: Leave them on, your coming with me.

CONSTABLE: Where's the fire?

SERGEANT: Picking up a couple of natives, Joe Millimurra and Mary…

He reads the desk and copies the name onto a scrap of paper.

Darg… something.

CONSTABLE: What for?

SERGEANT: Absconding. Council, George Withnall and Ray Brew and so on have been getting on the Chief Protector's back. [*Starting to search*] Do you know where those warrants for their removal are?

CONSTABLE: Haven't seen them for months. What's the panic? They've been here for weeks.

SERGEANT: Oh, you know all this Royal Commission business. Some mob of do-gooder women are kicking up about them being shifted out before the election.

He finds the warrants.

You can stop looking now, Constable… [*reading*] 'Lawrence'… 'Lawson'… 'Millimurra'. Come on. Royal Commission on Natives; they had one about thirty years ago. A waste of bloody time, like the bloody referendum; they'll just stick it in some government filing cabinet and forget about it.

SCENE FOUR

A street in Northam, day. JOE *is approached by* SERGEANT CARROL *and* CONSTABLE KERR.

SERGEANT: G'day, Joe. Where's the girl?
JOE: What girl?
CONSTABLE: Don't be smart, just answer the question.
JOE: Don't have to be smart to answer your questions.
SERGEANT: Where is she?
JOE: What do you want her for?
CONSTABLE: Listen, you cheeky bla—
SERGEANT: [*interrupting*] I'll handle this. Come on, Joe, where is she?
JOE: Out at Lockyers.
SERGEANT: You are under arrest under Section Twelve of the Aborigines Act for absconding from the Moore River Settlement with, urn…

He takes the piece of paper out of his pocket and peruses it.

JOE: What for? We're not livin' in town.
SERGEANT:… With Mary Dargurru.
JOE: Why are youse worryin' about us now? We been back in Northam for nearly two months.
SERGEANT: Because Mr Neville only contacted me this morning.
JOE: What about Mary?
SERGEANT: The girl? She'll be returned to the settlement.
JOE: Back to that bastard.
SERGEANT: What do you mean by that?
JOE: It's my business.
CONSTABLE: Hold out your hands.

He produces handcuffs.

JOE: You ain't puttin' them on me.
CONSTABLE: Are you resisting arrest?
JOE: No I'm not… I just don't want them things on me.
SERGEANT: [*to the* CONSTABLE] Don't worry about them. If he runs he'll only get an extra couple of months.
JOE: I'm not gunna run.
SERGEANT: Take him down the lock-up.
JOE: Sergeant, will you tell Mary where I am? She's out at Lockyers, on the York Road.

SERGEANT: Yeah, I know. I'll tell her.

The SERGEANT *exits.*

CONSTABLE: Come on, get movin'.

JOE *doesn't move.*

Get movin'!

JOE: I'm not walkin' in front of you.

CONSTABLE: Why not?

JOE: You're not the sort of bloke I want to turn me back to.

They walk off slowly, side by side.

SCENE FIVE

AUBER OCTAVIUS NEVILLE, *groomed and dressed smartly, addresses the Royal Western Australian Historical Society. Behind him is a portrait of the King, the Union Jack and the Western Australian flag. He nears the end of a long speech.*

NEVILLE: Ladies and gentlemen of the Historical Society, it has been a great privilege and pleasure to address you here tonight at a time when, with Mr Mosley's Royal Commission, the welfare of our Aboriginal and coloured folk is somewhat more than usually in the public arena. If I may beg your indulgence for a few more minutes, I shall conclude with a brief word about those early years when that little band of pioneers, fewer than one hundred souls, led by Captain Stirling, laid anchor in the Swan River, little knowing that they faced in the fertile valleys of the South-West alone some thirteen thousand savages. Stirling's first acts was to issue a proclamation regarding the treatment of the native inhabitants.

He reads:

'And whereas the protection of the law doth of right belong to all people whatsoever who may come or be found within the territory aforesaid, I do hereby give notice that if any person or persons shall be, convicted of behaving in a fraudulent, cruel, or felonious manner towards the aboriginal race of inhabitants of this country, such a person or persons will be liable to be prosecuted and tried for the offence as if the same had been committed against any others of

His Majesty's subjects.' In the same proclamation, all male persons between the ages of fifteen and fifty were required to enrol in the militia, to secure the safety of the territory from invasion and from the attacks of hostile native tribes as might be necessary.

Pause.

From the beginning the natives provided the settlers with bush food and assisted exploring parties, and a happy relationship between settlers and blacks continued for some eighteen months. The newcomers were yet to impress the blacks with the significance of their invasion. In November of that year, an Aborigine was shot while stealing flour. That was the beginning of the end. Constant pressure from the whites drove back the erstwhile native inhabitants, depriving them of their water and food supplies. Naturally enough, the bolder spirits among the blacks resented this, and we cannot wonder that the murder of isolated whites occurred during this period, with a heavy toll of black life being exacted in reprisal. On the twenty-seventh of October, 1834, Governor Stirling led a detachment of soldiers and civilians to the Murray River at Pinjarra. In the early morning they came across a camp of some sixty or seventy natives. The detachment took up positions on both sides of the river. Rain, which had been threatening for some time, began to fall heavily. The party opened fire and more natives appeared from shelters. The men defended themselves with spears, while the women and children sought shelter in the river. For one hour they were subjected to crossfire from twenty-four guns from both banks. The official estimate was fifteen to twenty dead, but only eight women and several children were finally rounded up.

He pauses and takes a drink of water.

One more word and I shall have finished. When referring to Australia's treatment of her Aborigines we are apt to refer somewhat scathingly to Tasmania's harshness in ridding herself of her natives within the first seventy years of settlement. In that time some six thousand natives disappeared and only one was left alive. Yet here, in the south-west of our State, within an area about twice the size of Tasmania between 1829 and 1901 seventy-two years—a people estimated to number thirteen thousand were reduced to one thousand four hundred and nineteen, of whom nearly half were half-caste.

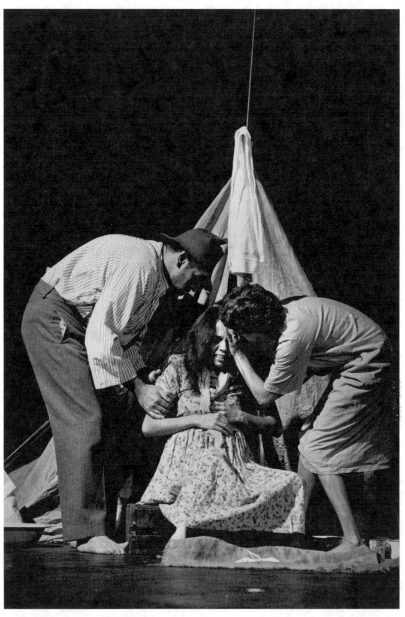

Morton Hansen with Jedda Cole as Mary and Lynette Narkle as Milly. Photo by Tony McDonough.

ACT FOUR, MOORE RIVER

SCENE ONE

Moore River outdoor Sunday School, a hot day. SISTER EILEEN, CISSIE *and* TOPSY *sit in a group.* SISTER EILEEN *is telling a story from memory. Next to her are several sheets of paper.*

SISTER: After the shepherds had visited the baby Jesus in the manger, Mary and Joseph and the Holy Jesus had three very special visitors. Can anyone tell me who they were?

TOPSY: The Three Wise Men, Sister Eileen.

SISTER: Yes, very good, Topsy. And the Three Wise Men brought the Holy Jesus gifts of gold, frankincense and myrrh. But on the way to visit Jesus the Three Wise Men spoke to the King of Judea. Who can tell me the name of the King of Judea?

> TOPSY*'s hand goes up.*

Well, do you know, Cissie?

CISSIE: No, Sister.

SISTER: Topsy, can you tell us?

TOPSY: King Herod, Sister.

> CISSIE *notices* DAVID *enter at a distance.* BILLY *enters behind* DAVID *and sees him.*

SISTER: That's right, King Herod. And when the Three Wise Men heard that a Saviour was born to be King of the Jews, he wasn't pleased at all, because he was king and he didn't want any other king. So what did he do? Can anybody tell me?

> BILLY *puts a hand on* DAVID*'s shoulder.* CISSIE *puts up her hand.*

BILLY: Eh, boy, where you goin'?

DAVID: Swimmin'.

SISTER: [*surprised*] Yes, Cecilia.

> BILLY *belts* DAVID *on the legs with his whip.*

CISSIE: Look, Sister Eileen, look.

BILLY: [*to* DAVID] You s'posed to be Chunday School. *Gudeeah* waitin'
   for you.

TOPSY: Billy Kimberley's belting one of the boys.

BILLY: [*to* DAVID] Now you git to Sunday School, straight away now,
   git, git, git.

CISSIE: It's David.

   She jumps up and picks up a stone, and runs to DAVID.

SISTER: Cecilia, wait. Cecilia!

   SISTER EILEEN *jumps up and runs after her.*

CISSIE: You leave him alone, old man.

SISTER: Billy, Billy!

   CISSIE *prepares to throw the stone.*

Cecilia, don't you dare!

   She grabs CISSIE*'s arm.*

Billy, what are you hitting that boy for?

BILLY: Him cheeky fella, missus. He goin' swimmin', don't wanna go
   Chunday school. He bad boy, that one.

SISTER: All right, Billy, but we don't hit people to make them do God's
   will.

DAVID: [*to* BILLY] Black crow, black crow.

SISTER: David, that's enough of that! Come on, now.

BILLY: [*to* DAVID] You bad boy.

   He exits.

SISTER: Did he hurt you?

DAVID: I'm all right.

CISSIE: Rotten stinkin' mongrel.

SISTER: That's enough! David, in one way it's your own fault.

DAVID: It's not.

SISTER: If you'd been at Sunday School that wouldn't have happened,
   so remember that... All right, now where were we?

   She gives DAVID *a humbug and they go back to the others.*

TOPSY: King Herod, Sister Eileen.

SISTER: Now, King Herod was very angry and very wicked and you
   know what he did? He ordered his soldiers to kill every first-born

baby boy under two years old. So Mary and Joseph didn't want
them to kill the baby Jesus, so they had to flee from Bethlehem.
They wrapped the baby in a blanket and crept away in the middle
of the night. They travelled all night and by sunrise they were far
away and safe.

TOPSY: Where did they go, Sister?

SISTER: They went to Egypt until King Herod died and there was a new
King of Judea. And then they returned to Jesus' home in Nazareth,
where Jesus grew up to be a man. Now wasn't that a splendid story?
Did you like it, David?

DAVID: S'all right.

SISTER EILEEN *hands out a sheet of paper to each.*

SISTER: Now, here are the hymn sheets for today. It's a hymn I'm sure
you all know, and want you to sing in your very best voice, because
this is the hymn we'll be singing for Mr Neville in the Australia Day
celebrations.

ALL: [*singing*]
> There is a happy land,
> Far, far away,
> Where saints in glory stand,
> Bright, bright as day:
> Oh, how they sweetly sing,
> 'Worthy is our Saviour King!'
> Loud, let His praises ring,
> Praise, praise for aye!
>
> Bright in that happy land,
> Beams every eye:
> Kept by a Father's hand
> Love cannot die.
> Oh, then, to glory run,
> Be a Crown and Kingdom won
> And, bright above the sun,
> Reign, reign for aye!
> Amen.

They gather around for their humbugs. DAVID *holds out his
hand.*

CISSIE: You've already had one.

DAVID: Shut up.

> SISTER EILEEN *gives him a humbug.*

SCENE TWO

The Superintendent's Office, Moore River, day. MR NEAL *reads at his desk.* MATRON *enters while* BILLY *and* MARY, *now very pregnant, wait outside.*

MATRON: She's here.

NEAL: Dargurru?

MATRON: Yes.

NEAL: Oh, good. Aren't you needed down the hospital?

MATRON: Just remember, that girl is pregnant, and unwell.

NEAL: Don't worry, I won't touch her.

> MATRON *exits.*

NEAL: Billy? Billy?

BILLY: Yes, boss.

NEAL: Bring her in.

> BILLY *brings* MARY *into the office.*

You wait, all right? Don't go walkabout.

> BILLY *goes outside to wait.*

Dargurru, you finally got caught, eh? And you got yourself pregnant? Well, you'll be all right here. You can stay in the nurses' quarters.

MARY: No, I wanta stay with Joe's Mum and Dad.

NEAL: Don't be stupid, girl: you're meant to be pregnant and sick, so you can stay in the nurses' quarters and do a bit of light work in the hopsital.

MARY: I don't want to work in the hospital.

NEAL: You'll work where I think fit, digging graves if I say so.

MARY: I'm not gunna work in the hospital.

NEAL: You'll do as I say, do you understand?

MARY: No.

NEAL: So you intend to defy me, do you? Billy!

> *He takes the cat-o'-nine-tails from his desk.*

Do you know what that is?

BILLY *enters.*

MARY: I don't care. You can belt me if you like, I'm not workin' in the hospital.

BILLY: Boss talkin' to you.

MARY: Go to hell!

BILLY: Don't be cheeky, now.

NEAL: [*to* MARY] What did you say?

Silence.

BILLY: Boss talkin' to you.

NEAL: What— did— you— say?

MARY: Go to hell! Fuck youse!

NEAL: Millimurra seems to have learnt her well. Well, I'm going to unlearn you.

NEAL *grabs her.* BILLY *holds her outstretched over a pile of flour bags.* NEAL *raises the cat-o'-nine-tails. Blackout. A scream.*

SCENE THREE

Long Pool Camp, Moore River. MILLY *sorts clothes for washing.* SAM *and* JIMMY *drink tea.* GRAN *sits in the shade.* MILLY *looks up as* MARY *enters.*

MILLY: Mary! Oh, gawd, Mary…

MILLY *runs to her, takes the flour and helps her to the camp.*

Come on, Mary, sit down.

MARY *sits painfully.*

You all right?

MARY: Yeah.

The others gather around as MILLY *carefully lifts the back of* MARY's *galatea blouse to reveal huge welts.* GRAN *fetches some medicinal leaves.*

SAM: Oh, my gawd.

JIMMY: The bastard. I'll kill him.

GRAN: Ne'mine, ne'mine, put these *jeerung meear* on your back. Fix up quick and make you better.

MILLY: Baby all right?

MARY: Yeah. He's kickin' like a Kimberley camel.

SAM: I think we better take her to the hospital.

MARY: No. No, I'm not goin' to no hospital. I'll die first.

MILLY: But you'll have to go to have the baby.

MARY: No, I'm havin' it 'ere. I can 'ave it 'ere, can't I?

GRAN: You can have it right 'ere, darlin'. I brought Joe into this world and, by crikey, I'll bring his baby.

The sound of the shrill voices of DAVID *and* CISSIE *are heard, off.*

DAVID and CISSIE: [*together*] Mum, Dad…

The kids run on. DAVID *carries a letter.*

CISSIE: Mary, a letter from Brother Joe.

MARY *takes the letter and reads.*

DAVID: Willy Knapp give it to me. He just came back from gaol, and Joe give it to him.

CISSIE: Gave it to him, not 'give'.

DAVID: That's what I said.

CISSIE: *Nyummi.*

DAVID:… Give it him to gave to youse so Mr Neal wouldn't read it and tear it up or something.

JIMMY: Bastard reads everybody's mail.

MILLY: How is he?

MARY: Good, reckons the tucker's all right. Here, you read it, Cissie.

CISSIE *takes the letter and reads in silence.*

DAVID: Out loud, *nyummi*!

CISSIE: 'I'm giving this to Willie to give to youse 'coz if…'

Pause.

[*Spelling*] 'F-U-C-K F-A-C-E gets it, he'll most likely tear it up. How is everyone? Mum and Dad and Gran and the kids and Uncle Jimmy… And my little brother and sister? But really, how are you and the baby? I've only got eight weeks to go and I'm counting them days, every one of them. We are getting married when I get out. If the Aborigines Department give us permission. I am going to ask Mister Neville myself. I'd sooner we got married at New Norcia like Mum and Dad. Though I ain't really a Catholic. You know, I

don't know what you are, I forgot to ask you. It not too bad here, plenty of Nyoongahs and some from up North. Tucker's not too bad, better than the Settlement. At least they don't give us bread and fat, and we get real 'bacca, not nigger twist. Tell Willy to behave himself now he's out and not to go hitting any more policemen.
  Well, darling, I'll close.

CISSIE *sniggers.*

'I love you and I think of you day and night.'

She laughs.

'I even dream about you. Lots of love and kisses to you and Baby. Joe.'

MILLY: Come on, Mary, you come and lie down.

SCENE FOUR

The Superintendent's Office, Moore River. MR NEAL *works at his desk.* SISTER EILEEN *approaches and knocks. He ignores it. She knocks again.*

NEAL: Who is it?
SISTER: Me, Sister Eileen.

> *He continues working, head down.* SISTER EILEEN *enters the office.*

Matron said you wanted to see me.
NEAL: Yeah.

> *He continues working. Pause.*

Yeah, now… Australia Day, the ceremony. Mr Neville likes to have the agenda in advance. I'd like you to say a few words yourself and an appropriate hymn.
SISTER: We've been practising 'There Is a Happy Land'… I thought it would be…
NEAL: Good.
SISTER: I thought it might be nice if Mr Neville announced the hymn.
NEAL: Yeah, all right. What was it again?
SISTER: 'There Is a Happy Land'.

> NEAL *writes it down and shuffles his papers. He ignores her. Pause.*

Is that all, Mr Neal?

NEAL: Just a moment… There's another matter I'd like to discuss with you. I believe you've been lending books—novels—to some of the natives.

SISTER: Yes, I have.

NEAL: There's a sort of unofficial directive on this; it's the sort of thing which isn't encouraged by the Department.

SISTER: What do you mean? That you don't encourage the natives to read?

NEAL: That's right.

SISTER: [*incredulously*] But why? I'd intended to ask your permission to start a small library.

NEAL: I'm sorry, Sister, but—

SISTER: [*interrupting*] It won't cost the Department a penny, I can get the books donated. Good books.

NEAL: It's quite out of the question.

SISTER: But why?

NEAL: Look, my experience with natives in South Africa and here has taught—led me to believe that there's a lot of wisdom in the old adage that 'a little knowledge is a dangerous thing'.

SISTER: I can't believe what you're saying.

NEAL: Look Sister, I've got a big mob here, over seven hundred—you know that—and there's enough troublemakers without giving them ideas.

SISTER: But Mr Neal—

NEAL: [*interrupting*] I don't think there's anything more to be said on the subject.

SISTER: Well, I'd like to say something on another subject.

NEAL: Yes?

SISTER: The use of violence by your native policemen to enforce attendance at my religious instruction classes.

NEAL: If I didn't make attendance compulsory, you'd have none of them there.

SISTER: I'd prefer that they come of their own free will.

NEAL: Look, Sister, if you're not happy here, I could arrange a transfer for you to another settlement; perhaps Mulla Bulla, on the edge of the Gibson Desert.

She goes to leave, but stops by the door.

SISTER: Getting back to the books, what do you classify the Bible as?

She exits.

NEAL: [*To himself*] Bloody do-gooders.

SCENE FIVE

Moore River Native Settlement, Australia Day, 1934, a very hot afternoon. MR NEVILLE, MR NEAL *and* MATRON *are seated on a dais.* BILLY KIMBERLEY *and* BLUEY, *dressed in new but absurdly ill-fitting uniforms, stand beside a flag pole with a flag furled ready to raise.* SISTER EILEEN *addresses the assembled population of the settlement, including the Millimurra family.* JOE *is still absent.*

SISTER: It gives me great pleasure to be with you all on this very special day, when we gather together to pledge our allegiance to the King and to celebrate the birth of this wonderful young country that we are so fortunate to be living in. We must remember today not just our country and King, but the King of kings, the Prince of princes, and to give thanks to God for what He has provided for us because our sustenance in life is provided by Him. Even we here today, Mr Neal, Matron Neal and myself, are but His humble servants, sent by Him to serve your needs. The Lord Jesus Christ has sent His servant, Mr Neville, Chief Protector of Aborigines, to speak to us on this special day. Mr Neville is going to say a few words before leading us in a song of praise to our Lord and Saviour, Jesus Christ.

> NEVILLE *rises. The whites clap while the Aborigines remain silent.*

NEVILLE: Today we are gathered here to celebrate the birth of this nation of Australia one hundred and forty-six years ago at Sydney Cove in the Eastern States. As I was driving up, I remembered that it is only a hundred and four years since the British flag was first raised on our West Australian shores. As I drove through Guildford, Midland and Bullsbrook, I saw men on the road, hundreds of men, and I was reminded that the world is in the grip of depression and that many people are suffering from hunger and deprivation of many of the essential elements which make for a contented existence. But you, in this small corner of the Empire, are fortunate in being provided for with adequate food and shelter.

JIMMY: [*muttering*] Yeah, weevily flour.

NEVILLE:... And to be with family and friends. Occasionally some of you might ponder why you are here—

JIMMY: [*a little louder*] Too bloody right.

SAM: [*to* JIMMY] *Dubakieny wahnginy, gnoolya.*

NEVILLE:... It doesn't hurt to remind yourselves that you are preparing yourselves here to take your place in Australian society, to live as other Australians live, and to live alongside other Australians; to learn to enjoy the privileges and to shoulder the responsibilities of living like the white man, to be treated equally, not worse, not better, under the law.

> *Pause. He looks around at the others on the dais.*

SAM: What's he talkin' about?

JIMMY: He's talkin' outa his *kwon.*

SISTER: [*aside, to* NEVILLE] The hymn.

NEVILLE: We are now going to sing the song... ah, hymn.

NEAL: [*aside to* NEVILLE] The hymn, then the flag raising.

NEVILLE: Sing the hymn before we raise the flag and sing the national anthem. [*To* SISTER EILEEN] Sorry, I've forgotten.

SISTER: 'There is a Happy Land'.

NEVILLE: 'There is a Happy Land'.

> SISTER EILEEN *stands.*

ALL: [*singing*]
> There is a happy land,
> Far, far away,
> Where saints in glory stand,
> Bright, bright as day:
> Oh, how they sweetly sing,
> 'Worthy is our Saviour King!'
> Loud let His praises ring,
> Praise, praise for aye!

> *As the whites continue, the Aborigines break into full clear voice with a parody of the words.*

There is a happy land,
Far, far away.
No sugar in our tea,
Bread and butter we never see.
That's why we're gradually
Fading away.

NEVILLE: Stop, stop. Stop that immediately.

The Aborigines repeat the parody even louder.

Stop it. Stop this nonsense immediately. Never in my life have I witnessed such a disgraceful exhibition.

The song stops.

I'm appalled by this disgraceful demonstration of ingratitude. I can tell you that you will live to rue this day. There will be no privileges from now on.

JIMMY: [*calling out*] Rotten spuds and onions?

NEVILLE: Be quiet! And there will be no Christmas this year! No Christmas!

JIMMY: What, a dried up orange and a puddin'?

NEVILLE: Will you be quiet? Who is it, who is that fellow? Munday, isn't it? Northam. I've got police reports on you. You're a troublemaker, and a ringleader. You must listen to me.

JIMMY: [*approaching* NEVILLE] No, you listen to me Mr A.O. You come an' eat supper with us, tonight, right? Bread and drippin' and black tea. Are you game to try it?

NEAL *stands to leave, then turns back.*

NEAL: Look, Munday, what's your bloody game?

JIMMY: Did you vote for Jimmy Mitchell's lot?

Silence. JIMMY *sniggers.* SISTER EILEEN *stands and starts to sing 'God Save the King'. The other whites join in. The Aborigines laugh.*

Yeah, you musta done, eh?

NEAL *stares at him in disbelief. The blacks, with the exception of the Millimurra family, gradually disperse.* BILLY *and* BLUEY *remain by the flag.*

Nothin' to do with bloody scabies. And that's why we got dragged 'ere; so them *wetjalas* vote for him.

JIMMY is left alone, shouting. SAM *looks on.*

So he could have a nice, white little town, a nice, white little fuckin' town.

JIMMY runs out of breath, heaves and clutches his chest. SAM *catches him as he collapses, clutching at the flagpole. The official party continues to sing 'God Save the King'.* JIMMY's *family rushes to him.*

MARY: Matron, Matron, help! Help us!

NEAL: [*to the whites*] Ah! He's only fainted.

The singing stops. MATRON *breaks ranks and rushes to* JIMMY's *aid, loosens his clothing, checks his breathing and pulse.*

MATRON: He's got a heart condition. Billy, Bluey, pick him up. Bring him to the hospital. Come on, come on. Easy now.

MATRON and the Millimurras exit with BILLY *and* BLUEY. *NEVILLE and NEAL exit in the other direction.* SISTER EILEEN *remains, unsure which way to go.*

SCENE SIX

The Superintendant's Office, day. NEAL *reads the West Australian, Monday 30 January 1934.* MATRON *enters.*

MATRON: What's the latest?

NEAL: A cool change tomorrow.

He looks at the date on the paper.

That's today.

MATRON: Not much sign of it.

NEAL: Pictures of cars stuck in the bitumen on Crawley Drive. Hmm, a truck load of eggs in Fremantle hatched out chickens… Hot, all right.

MATRON: No news from Kalgoorlie?

NEAL: Oh, yeah… Three dead.

MATRON: Oh, dear.

NEAL: Yeah, besides Jordan. One of us stabbed—typical—and one a them shot. The foreigners have dug themselves in around Ding Flat… They're recruiting specials.

MATRON: Who?

NEAL: Volunteers, special constables. A man with a military background has a responsibility to volunteer in an emergency like this.

MATRON: Why don't you?

NEAL: Can't leave this place.

> MILLY *and* SAM *approach the office.*

MATRON: Got your own civil war?

NEAL: Don't be stupid, woman, I can handle a mob of unruly niggers.

MATRON: Yes? Yes, Milly? Hello, Sam.

MILLY: [*pointing inside*] We want to see him.

> MATRON *beckons them in.*

NEAL: [*to* SAM *and* MILLY] What do you want?

SAM: We want to know if you can get Joe out for the funeral.

NEAL: Who?

MATRON: Joe Millimurra.

NEAL: Impossible.

MILLY: Why? Other Nyoongahs get out when the 'lations die.

SAM: You could ring up Mr Neville and ask him.

NEAL: Too late. Funeral's tomorrow.

SAM: Well, hold it the day after.

NEAL: What, in this weather?

MILLY: You could if you wanted to.

> MILLY *starts to cry.*

MATRON: Don't get upset; there's nothing we can do about it.

MILLY: And don't you go wrappin' him up in the gubment blanket. You put him in a proper box.

MATRON: Don't worry, he'll receive a proper burial.

SAM: Will you ring the prison and tell 'em to tell Joe?

NEAL: As a member of the family you can write to him yourself.

MILLY: You scared to tell him. You scared to tell him.

> SAM *puts his hands on her shoulders and tries to steer her to the door.* MILLY *struggles against him.*

You're scared' to tell him. You're scared at what he'll do when he gets out. You're *wayarniny. Wayarniny bridaira*, you're *wayarniny*.

SAM: Come on, Milly, we get Cissie to write to him. Come on, Milly.

Come on, come on now.

MILLY: I'll tell him all about it when he gits out, you hear me? You hear me?

SAM: Come on, Mil, *dubakieny*.

MILLY: An' Matron, you don't forget put him in a proper coffin box, Matron. Matron, coo-cooo, cooh.

They exit.

NEAL: [*to* MATRON] A classic case of emotion comes in through the door and reason goes out the window.

MATRON: [*exiting*] I couldn't agree more. Seems to be happening frequently in this office lately.

SCENE SEVEN

Long Pool Camp, Moore River, night. The campfire is blazing. DAVID *is asleep.* MARY, GRAN *and* MILLY *are silhouetted inside the tent.* MARY *suffers a contraction.*

MARY: Help, help! Joe! I want Joe!

The contraction continues.

Don't let them take Baby. Don't let them take Baby.

She cries in panic.

GRAN: Nobody's goin' to take Baby, darlin'. Nobody. You'll be all right, darling, Matron comin' to see you directly.

MARY: I don't want her to come here. Granny, tell her to go away. Please, I don't want to see her.

GRAN: You shut up, now. What will Joe say if anythin' happens to you and Baby, eh? We gotta look after youse.

MARY: I wish Joe was here.

Another contraction starts and she yells.

GRAN: [*to* MILLY] Gawd, I think it's comin'. [*To* MARY] Come on darlin', push down. Come on, breathe deep.

The contraction continues.

[*To* MILLY] Git the water and the rags. [*To* MARY] Come on darlin', you doin' good. Joe'd be real *tjeuri piny* for you. Breathe deep, eh? [*To* MILLY] Git me clean ashes, make sure there's no lumps.

> MARY *cries out while* MILLY *collects ashes on a sugar bag, picking out the pieces of charcoal. She takes the ashes, water and rags back to the tent.*

Come on, darlin', breathe deep. Push down, keep pushin', keep pushin'. Hurry up, Milly, come on. [*To* MARY] Come on, darlin', you doin' good.

> MARY *yells and sighs.*

Firestick! Firestick, live one, quick!

> MILLY *races to the fire and takes a burning stick back into the tent.*

I got you a little Nyoongah. Now I cut your cord and tie it, make a real pretty belly button for you, just like your daddy's. Now cover you in ashes. More better than Johnson's Baby Powder, eh?

> *The baby cries.*

You got a great big handsome Nyoongah boy. Come on, darlin', one more push, come on…

> MARY *pushes.*

Keep pushin', eh? Good, it's all over.

> DAVID *wakes.*

GRAN: There you are, darlin'. He's yours for life.
DAVID: Hey? What's goin' on?
MILLY: You're an uncle now.
DAVID: What? Dinkum?

> DAVID *rushes to the tent and looks in.*

Geez, look at him. Why don't he open his *meeowl*?
MILLY: 'Coz he's just been born, son. He's only five minutes old.

> SAM *appears, breathless.*

Where's Matron?
SAM: They comin'.
DAVID: We don't need her, everything's all right.
SAM: Dinkum?
GRAN: That's what David said.
SAM: Here's Matron comin' now.

MATRON *appears with a hurricane lamp and a satchel followed by* CISSIE *and* TOPSY.

MATRON: Hello, Granny. Hello everybody.

MARY: No! Don't let Matron see Baby. Granny, go and hide him. Please, please, don't let Matron take him away.

The three approach the tent.

MATRON: Well, well. How is she? Hello, Mary.

GRAN: Baby boy.

CISSIE: Oh, he's beautiful.

MATRON: Come on, Mary, don't be a silly girl. I just want to check him over.

MARY: No, don't touch him! You're not havin' my baby, leave him alone!

MATRON: But Mary, it's for your own good and the baby's and I only want to help.

MARY: No, don't take him to hospital. The trackers will get him and kill him.

MATRON: What on earth is she talking—

MARY: [*interrupting*]… And bury him in the pine plantation.

MATRON: I think she's delirious.

MARY: Like Lillian's baby. Mr Neal tell them to do it, to kill Baby.

MATRON: She's delirious.

SAM: No she ain't.

MARY: Gran, Gran, don't let 'em take him.

GRAN: [*soothingly*] No one's takin' Baby, darlin'. You're all right, you're all right. [*To* MATRON] She's all right. Better go.

MATRON: Gran evidently seems to have done a good job.

GRAN: I brought plenty of babies into this world, Matron.

MATRON: [*reaching into her satchel*] Well, here's plenty of clean cotton wool and baby powder and Lysol soap.

GRAN: Don't need powder, use me own.

MATRON: All right, see you tomorrow when she's calmed down. [*To* MARY] Bye, dear. You have a good sleep now.

MARY: Yes, Matron.

MATRON *and* TOPSY *leave the tent and vanish into the darkness with the hurricane lamp.*

SCENE EIGHT

Long Pool Camp, Moore River, day. GRAN *seems to have aged suddenly. She sits and stares into the smouldering fire, quietly grumbling and singing.* CISSIE *and* DAVID *play knucklebones.* MILLY *and* SAM *play cards.* MARY *watches over the baby who sleeps in a kerosene tin. A loud whistle is heard in the distance.*

SAM: Who the hell is that?
DAVID: Boys whistling at girls, I bet.
MARY: No.

    The whistle is heard again.

I know that whistle, that's Joe. It's Joe, it's Joe!

    CISSIE *and* DAVID *start to run.*

MILLY: Come back, you two! Come back!
DAVID: It's Joe, Mum. It's Joe.

    The kids run off.

JOE: [*off*] Hey! Where are all you blackfellas?

    JOE *enters carrying a sugar bag and with* DAVID *on his back. They are followed by* CISSIE. *He sees* MARY *and they embrace. He swings her around and around.* DAVID *falls off, laughing and yelling.* JOE *wears a yellow shirt and black pants.*

How's everybody? Gawd, it's good to be back.
SAM: Yeah, son, we wasn't expectin' you for another two weeks.
DAVID: [*yelling, pointing to the tin*] Your baby in there! [*Quietly*] Sleepin'.
JOE: How are you, Gran?
GRAN: Bit crook. [*Rubbing her leg*] Me leg git tired, little bit, this one.
MARY: Come and see baby.

    They walk to where the baby sleeps.

JOE: Gawd.

    Pause.

Can he sit up?
MARY: Give him time. He's only ten weeks old.

JOE: What did you call him?
SAM: We call him *koolbardi*, Nyoongah name.
GRAN: Magpie.
MARY: We waited for you to come home to give him a *wetjala* name.

Silence.

JOE: I wanna call him Jimmy.

Silence.

MARY: Yeah.

GRAN *begins to wail and cry.*

JOE: Eh, Gran, got somethin' here for you.

[*He dives his hand into the sugar bag and produces a wooden pipe and a tin of tobacco.*]

Here y'are, Gran, real pipe and real *gnummarri*, not nigger twist.
GRAN: *Woolah, kwobiduk, cooo-ooh.*
JOE: [*pulling out coloured ribbons*] Here y'are, Cissie, ribbons for your hair.
CISSIE: Oh thanks, brother, they're *moorditj*.

She ties yellow and red ribbons in her hair.

JOE: Here y'are, *gnoon.*

He gives DAVID a pocket knife.

Here y'are, Mum.

He produces a needle and cotton.

And Dad.

He produces tobacco and papers.

SAM: Hey, real papers. Rizlas. Good on ya, son.
MILLY: Didn't you git nothin' for Mary?
JOE: Course I did, Mum.

He pulls out a larger parcel and gives it to her.

Go on, open it.

She tears the paper off: it's a red dress.

MILLY: Go and try it on, dear.

SAM: Hey, son, where did you git the *boondah*?

JOE: Wages. Earned a few bob and they give it to me when I got out. Not like this place.

> *He takes out a packet of cigarettes.*

Had enough left for a packet of Luxor!

> *They share them.* MARY *returns with the dress on, unbuttoned down the back. She goes to* JOE *to do it up.*

Geez, what happened to your back?

MILLY: Neal belted her.

DAVID: With the cat-'o-nine-tails. Tracker held her down over the flour bags.

CISSIE: And she was seven months *bootjari*.

JOE: Dinkum?

GRAN: *Kunarn, kunarn!*

JOE: Bloody stinkin' walrus-faced bastard. I'm gunna kick his teeth down his fuckin' throat.

> *He starts to run off, but* MARY *stops him.*

MARY: Joe, please, please, please, don't go near him. Please think of Baby and me. He'll put you in gaol again.

JOE: But why did he have to belt you?

MARY: 'Cause I told him to go to hell.

JOE: Dinkum?

MARY: Yeah.

> *They embrace and laugh.*

He got wild 'coz I wouldn't knuckle under to him. Don't go, Joe, not now. Go on Monday and ask him if we can leave the Settlement. *Koodjie*'ll be there, an' he's scared a' her.

JOE: Who?

MARY: *Koodjie*. Matron. He's frightened a' her. Come an' see Uncle Herbie before Baby wakes; he's cruel hungry and he's got a cruel loud voice.

> *They exit.*

SCENE NINE

Superintendent's Office, Moore River, day. TOPSY *brings* NEAL *a cup of tea on a tray in exact repetition of Scene Five.* JOE *wails outside as* NEAL *rummages through drawers until he finds a piece of paper. He reads it, adds a few words, and places it on his desk.*

NEAL: [*yelling*] Millimurra!

> JOE *walks in, stands and stares at him in silence.*

Sign this.

JOE: What is it?

NEAL: Read it.

> JOE *takes the paper and reads it slowly to himself.*

Oh, Jesus, give it to me.

> *He snatches it from* JOE.

I want you to understand this. Are you listening?

JOE: I'm listenin'.

NEAL: 'I, Joseph Millimurra, undertake not to domicile in the town of Northam, nor anywhere in the Northam Shire. I fully understand that if I return to Northam I am liable to be returned under warrant to the Moore River or other Government Native Settlement.'

JOE: You mean if I put me name on this, me and Mary can take off?

NEAL: That's what I mean.

JOE: Right, give us the pen.

NEAL: Hold your horses. Billy! Billy!

BILLY: [*off*] Comin', boss. Comin'.

> BILLY *enters the office.*

NEAL: [*to* JOE] Witness.

JOE: Gawd, some witness.

BILLY: Yeah, boss?

NEAL: I want you to watch him sign this.

> NEAL *picks up the paper and shows it to* BILLY.

You can understand this?

BILLY: No, boss.

NEAL: Good. [*To* JOE] Go on, sign it.

JOE: [*signing*] Gawd, you *wetjalas* funny fellas.

NEAL: Good, now get out. The sooner you leave, the better.

JOE: [*leaving*] I'll see you one day, in hell. And you won't have your cat-o'-nine-tails.

> *He laughs and walks out with* BILLY.

BILLY: Hey, what that one *milly milly*?

JOE: Me an' Mary clearin' out, an' that one say we not allowed to go to Northam.

BILLY: Augh, *gudeeah*, silly fella.

JOE: If I go back to Northam he put me this one.

> *He puts his fingers across his face, indicating gaol.*

BILLY: That your country. You back sit down that place.

> MARY *enters with some baby clothes.*

MARY: Everything all right?

JOE: Couldn't be better.

MARY: What. happened?

JOE: He told us to get outa the Settlement.

MARY: When?

JOE: Tomorrow, next day, soon as we like.

MARY: Why?

JOE: 'Coz the bastard's scared of us.

BILLY: You watch this one, she go Kargudda but she still Oomboolgari girl.

JOE: She'll be all right.

BILLY: You want this one?

> *He hands him his whip.*

Kill rabbit, snake, *bungarra*.

JOE: No, Billy, that's yours.

BILLY: Ne'mine, ne'mine.

MARY: Take it, it's a gift.

JOE: Thanks, old man.

> JOE *walks off, leaving* BILLY *and* MARY *together.*

MARY: Goodbye, *dumbart*.

JOE: [*returning to* BILLY] Here, *gnummari*.

He gives BILLY *the rest of his packet of Luxor.* BILLY *breaks one up and puts it in his pipe. He gazes at them as they walk off.*

NEAL: [*off*] Billy!

BILLY: Comin' boss. Comin'.

He exits.

SCENE TEN

Long Pool Camp, Moore River, morning. The fire is burning. JOE *rolls a swag.* MILLY *gives* MARY *a sugar bag. The others stand around.*

MILLY: There's enough flour there for three dampers, a fryin' pan, billy can and two mugs. A bit of drippin', too, and a spud and a couple a' onions.

MARY: Thanks, Mum.

SAM: Where will you go, son?

JOE: Back to Northam.

GRAN: You wanna watch them *manatj*, they *warrah* there now.

JOE: Yeah, Gran. Don't worry, if they git rough we just move on.

MARY *straps the baby to her chest.*

GRAN: Just as well you a good milker, girl. Least he won't go 'ungry.

CISSIE: You got him right next to the tit.

DAVID: Eh, brother, you want my pocket knife? You might need it.

JOE: No, Brudge, I can use glass if I wanna gut a rabbit.

SAM *hands* JOE *a home-made knife.*

SAM: Here, son, take this one.

JOE: No, I'll be all right.

SAM: Take it. I can git another bit of steel and make another one. Here, take it.

Magpies squawk. GRAN *begins to sing. They farewell each member of the family, then walk off into the distance.*

GRAN: [*singing*]

Weert miny, jinna koorling, weert miny.
Jinna koorling
Wayanna, wayanna, wayanna,
Weert, miny, weert miny, weert miny.
Jinna koorling
Jinna koorling
Jinna koorling
Yay, yay, yay
Coo-oo-ooo-ooh.

THE END

TRANSLATIONS OF SONGS

JIMMY'S SONG

Look, who is this coming?
Crabs, crabs, crabs, crabs
In the river mouth,
They are coming in the river mouth, river mouth,
Coming in the river mouth.
Fish coming up the river,
Up the river, up the river,
Fish in the river mouth,
Fish in the river mouth,
Coming up, coming up, coming up,
Fish and crabs, fish and crabs, fish and crabs,
Shout of praise!

GRAN'S SONG

Woe, woe, woe.
My boy and girl and baby
Going a long way walking,
That way walking,
That way walking.
Pity, pity, pity,
Hungry, walking, hungry,
Pity, pity, pity,
Hungry, hungry,
Walking, walking, walking,
Yay, yay, yay,
Cooo-ooo-ooo-oooh.

NOTES AND GLOSSARY OF ABORIGINAL TERMS

The Aboriginal language used in these plays is usually called *Nyoongah* but occasionally referred to as *Bibbulumun*. *Nyoongah* literally means 'man', but has become a general term denoting Aboriginality in the South-West of Western Australia. *Bibbulumun* is one of the fourteen South-West languages that have combined over the last 152 years to create the modern *Nyoongah* spoken in the play.

Nyoongah words here are spelt phonetically, however the pronunciations of certain sounds are as follows:

> NG has a silent 'g', as in 'sing'
> Y is always short, as in yet
> A is always long, as in 'raft'
> R is rolled, as with a Scottish burr
> TJ is pronounced 'ch', as in 'change'
> B is pronounced 'p', as in 'pit'

ALLEWAH, watch out
BAAL NOONINY BARMINY, he'll hit you
BARKINY, bite
BARMINY, strike
BILBARL, black goanna
BOOLYADUK, magic man
BOONDAH, money
BOOTJARRI, pregnant
BRIDAIRA, boss
BRUDGE, brother (from the English)
BUNGARRU, goanna
CHOO, shame
CHUBEL, spear
CLAPSTICKS, two short sticks which, when struck together give a
    musical beat for the corroborree
DAITJ, meat
DAWARRA, bad mouth
DAWARRA, NITJA WETJALA, bad mouth, this is a white man
DING, Italian (W.A. slang)
DOAK, throwing stick

DOOTHOO, dogs
DUBAKIENY, steady, slowly
DUBAKIENY WAHNGINY, talk steady
DUGAITJ, dugite snake
DUMBART, people of the same tribe
FREED, Fremantle, Fremantle Gaol (W.A. slang)
GNEEAN BAAL?, Who's he?
GNEEAN NITJA KOORLING?, Who's coming there? GNUNY, me, I
GNUNY TJENNA MINDITJ, my feet hurt
GNOOLYA, brother-in-law
GNOON, brother
GNUMMARRI, tobacco
GUDEEAH, white people, white person
GUGJA, lilyroot (North-West language)
INJI STICKS, decorated sticks used in the corroborree
JEERUNG MEEAR, medicinal leaves
KAAL, fire
KAEP, water
KARGUDDA, south
KIA, yes
KIENYA, shame
KILLARLA, tobacco (North-West language)
KONGI, uncle
KOODJIE, bony, the Sister and Matron's nickname
KOOLANGAH, children
KOOLBARDI, magpie
KOOMP, urine
KOORAWOOROONG, an expression of disbelief
KOORIES, women (North-West language)
KOORT, weak
KOORT MINDITJ, weak heart
KULIYA, yes, (North-West language)
KUNARN, true
KWOMBINYARN, excellent
KWON, arse
KWONNA TJUELLARA, bony arse
MANATJ, police, black cockatoo

MEEOWL, eyes

MERRANG, flour, bread

MINDITJ, sick

MIRRI-UP, hurry

MIRRI-UP, MIRRI-UP. ALLEWAH KOORKANJERRI GNUNY NOONINY WOORT DININY, WOORT DININY, hurry, hurry. Watch out sheep, I'm going to cut your throat

MOORDITJ, good

MUMMARI, little spirit beings

NEMINE, corruption of 'never mind'

NIETJUK, why

NITJA BRIDAIR YORGAH KOORLING, the boss's woman is coming

NYOONGAH, Aboriginal, literally 'man' in the languages of the South West. Some time after 1829 it entered common usage as a term denoting Aboriginality, similar to *Wongai* in the eastern goldfields, *Yamatji* in the Murchison and *Koori* and *Murri* in the eastern states.

NYORN, pity

NYORN, WINYARN, pity, poor fellow

NYUMMI, slow learner

RIZLA'S, a brand of cigarette papers

SHOO-I, a shout or warning of evil

TJENNA, feet

TJENNA GUBBI, an Aboriginal secret executioner

TJEURIPINY, glad

TJINUNG, look

TJIRRUNG, fat

TJUELLARA, bony

UNNA?, Isn't it?

WADDI, club

WAH, where

WAHNGING, talk

WANBRU, blankets

WANMULLA, cannibals

WARRAH, WARRAHMUT, bad

WAYARNINY, frightened

WEE-AH, cry of grief, yes

WEERNY, weak

WETJALA, white person, a corruption of the English 'white fellow'

WILBRA, rabbit

WILGI, specially prepared paint for ceremonies

WINJAR, where, which way

WINJAR KAEP?, Where's water

WINYARN, poor fellow, weak-willed person

WOGGA, (coll.) a blanket made up of four or six wheat sacks sewn together.

WOOLAH, shout of praise

YAHLLARAH, group dance

YOKKI, shout of praise

YONGA, YONGARAH, kangaroo

YORGAH, woman, girl

YUART, nothing, no

YUMBAH, children (North-West language)

BACKGROUND READING

Moore River Native Settlement
One of the most vivid accounts of Aboriginal life at the time of
No Sugar is to be found in *Not Slaves Not Citizens* by Peter Biskup,
University of Queensland Press, 1973. Here is part of his account of
the Settlement:

> The land was unsuitable for cultivation. In summer there was
> an acute shortage of water, alleviated only by the fact that the
> inmates were "content to drink the river water which is slightly
> brackish". The settlement was constructed to house 200 inmates;
> after the transfer of the Carrolup Aborigines, in June 1922, it
> had a population of almost 400. In the customary official
> jargon, the inmates were "perfectly happy and contented", but
> anyone with eyes to see would have found little to substantiate
> this claim. Fenced compound, camp police and the settlement
> "boob" were a part of daily life. Compound inmates were not
> allowed to leave the compound without written permission
> from the superintendent or the matron, and outside visitors had
> to have similar approval. Association of adults and children
> was prohibited, even in the dining room, where there were
> separate sittings for women and children. Female inmates were
> subjected to particularly strict discipline. Girls under the age of
> fifteen were segregated from older girls who in turn were kept
> apart from women with young children. Children's dormitories
> were locked and bolted from the outside at six o'clock in the
> evening, even in summer. For the "camp" aborigines (those not
> housed in the compound) institutional care meant little more
> than a weekly ration of 1½ pounds of sugar, 8 pounds of flour,
> 4 ounces of tea, 1 stick of tobacco, and 3½ pounds of meat, mainly
> kangaroo or brush flesh caught by the aborigines themselves.
> Wages for work performed were nominal. The inmates were also
> allowed to buy, through the superintendent, such items as books,
> magazines, sewing material or "anything of improving nature".
> The education of the one hundred-odd settlement children was
> entrusted to one teacher. Boys who were not "likely to improve
> further" were put to work on the farm before they reached
> school-leaving age, while girls were sent to work in the sewing

room or in the kitchen. The spiritual welfare of the inmates was entrusted to a resident Church of England missionary but her work was hampered by recurring clashes with the superintendent who objected to her "familiarity subersive of discipline" and the "lack of dignity which is so essential in one making an attempt to uplift, control and bless this childish race".

It is hardly surprising that the southern part-Aborigines should have come to regard Moore River as a prison. Recaptured absconders were invariably sentenced to fourteen days of solitary confinement in the "boob". Habitual absconders were occasionally sentenced to imprisonment in the Fremantle gaol. Girls who became pregnant after being sent to service were sent back under warrant, together with the child—in some cases almost white. Still, it would be wrong to regard the settlement as a concentration camp, or even as a place of permanent segregation. The administration was genuinely convinced that the harsh measures, and in particular the separation of the children from the parents, were absolutely necessary if the young generation was to be uplifted and weaned away from its Aboriginal background.   (pp.156-57)

This book also contains an account of the character and career of A.O. Neville, including his antipathy towards missionaries and his book *Australia's Coloured Minority* which he wrote after his retirement. Biskup quotes Neville's conclusion:

> The native must be helped in spite of himself! Even if a measure
> of discipline is necessary it must be applied, but it can be applied
> in such a way as to appear to be a gentle persuasion... the end in
> view will justify the means employed.   (p.70)

There is also an account of his attempt in 1927 to establish in the Kimberleys a Home for Criminally Minded Natives; and the protest in 1930 by the Road Boards Association of W.A. against the re-opening of property for reserves where indigent Aborigines could live under the supervision of the Police. The scheme was abandoned, leading to incidents like the transfer of natives from Northam in 1933; and severe overcrowding at Moore River.   (p.164)

A fuller comment on A.O. Neville and his work may be found in G.C. Bolton's essay, 'Black and White After 1897' in *A New History of Western Australia* edited by C.T. Stannage, University of W.A. Press, 1981. In it Professor Bolton writes:

A considerably abler man than his predecessors, Neville dominated the working out of Aboriginal policy for a generation. As an administrator he was astute, gentlemanly and fully aware of the limitations on manoeuvre in a government department of lowly status and funding. His assessment of Aboriginal capacity reflected the conventional wisdom of his day, perceiving the Aborigines as most attractive when most remote from the mainstream of Australian society: "The uncivilized natives have a code of their own which is in a way superior to ours but which seems to disintegrate as soon as they get in touch with civilization."   (pp.137-38)

The 1933 Election and the Secession Vote

A description of the secession movement which led to a referendum at the electoral ballot in 1933; and of the election itself which 'turned with equal decisiveness against the State's foremost local patriot', may be found in *A Fine Country to Starve In* by G.C. Bolton, University of W.A. Press, 1972. He writes:

Not only was Sir James Mitchell's government beaten by the biggest election landslide in twenty years, but he himself and half his cabinet were thrust out of their seats in Parliament.

Sir James Mitchell was apparently amazed at this result, but Lady Mitchell was not. Going the rounds among the housewives of Northam, canvassing for her husband as she always did, she kept coming across old acquaintances who told her apologetically that this time they were giving Labor a go, because of the Depression . A.R.G. Hawke, the young Labor organizer contesting the seat... was a relative new-comer to the district, only five years over from South Australia, but he found the Northam voters tremendously eager for a change of government. "You could get a thousand to a meeting if you just stood in the street and rang a bell."   (p.256)

The Oombulgarri Massacre (Act Two Scene Six)
Billy's account of the massacre of his people in the Kimberley region is adapted from a repo. t of such a massacre by Daniel Evans, taken down verbatim by the novelist Randolph Stow and quoted in full in his book *To the Islands*, Picador, 1983.

Western Australian Historical Society (Act Three Scene Five)
Mr Neville's paper to the society is adapted from a paper delivered by him in 1936, in the possession of the society.

Mary's Punishment (Act Four Scene Two)
The origin of the incident of Mary's whipping is from evidence to the Moseley Royal Commission of 1934 by Annie Morrison:

> Sir, i have six children three boys three girls at moore river. they haven't enough to eat. Water soup no meat and bread and fat for breakfast and tea no green vegetables and fruit. they haven't Warm clothes for Winter my children have only one blanket between three of them Winter and summer i have been there and seen it. i hear some girls screaming in the office and the teachers said two trackers held the Girls feet over a sack of flour and Mr Neal Gave them a hiding and till tha wet them self we had to eat the flour after.

Further reading

Ronald M. and Catherine H. Berndt (eds.), *Aborigines of the West*, University of W.A. Press, 1979.

Adam Shoemaker, 'An Interview with Jack Davis' in *Westerly* No.4, December 1982.